NEGOTIATING TECHNIQUES IN INTERNATIONAL COMMERCIAL CONTRACTS

Negotiating Techniques in International Commercial Contracts

C. CHATTERJEE
*LLM (Cambridge), LLM (London),
PhD (London), Barrister*

LONDON AND NEW YORK

First published 2000 by Ashgate Publishing

Reissued 2018 by Routledge
2 Park Square, Milton Park, Abingdon, Oxon OX14 4RN
711 Third Avenue, New York, NY 10017, USA

Routledge is an imprint of the Taylor & Francis Group, an informa business

Copyright © C. Chatterjee 2000

All rights reserved. No part of this book may be reprinted or reproduced or utilised in any form or by any electronic, mechanical, or other means, now known or hereafter invented, including photocopying and recording, or in any information storage or retrieval system, without permission in writing from the publishers.

Notice:
Product or corporate names may be trademarks or registered trademarks, and are used only for identification and explanation without intent to infringe.

Publisher's Note
The publisher has gone to great lengths to ensure the quality of this reprint but points out that some imperfections in the original copies may be apparent.

Disclaimer
The publisher has made every effort to trace copyright holders and welcomes correspondence from those they have been unable to contact.

A Library of Congress record exists under LC control number: 00130123

ISBN 13: 978-1-138-70492-3 (hbk)
ISBN 13: 978-1-138-70488-6 (pbk)
ISBN 13: 978-1-315-20250-1 (ebk)

Contents

Table of Cases viii
Table of International Conventions and Resolutions x

1 Some Basic Concepts Fundamental to Negotiation of
  International Commercial Contracts 1
  1.1 Introduction 1
  1.2 What is Negotiation? 1
  1.3 Negotiation and Conflict 2
  1.4 What is not Negotiation 3
  1.5 The Environment of Negotiation 3
  1.6 Interdependence and Negotiation 4
  1.7 Professionalism in Negotiation 5
  1.8 Conclusions 6

2 Preparation for Negotiation 8
  2.1 Introduction 8
  2.2 Elements Common to the Preparatory Stages of Negotiation 8
  2.3 The Briefing Session 9
  2.4 The Stage Prior to Leaving for a Foreign Jurisdiction 11
  2.5 Eligibility for Membership of a Negotiating Team 12
  2.6 Conclusions 12

3 Negotiation of International Commercial Contracts and Risks 14
  3.1 Introduction 14
  3.2 Feasibility Studies 14
  3.3 A Brief Analysis of Some of the Usual Risks Associated with
      Private Foreign Investments 16
  3.4 The Primary Causes of High Incidence of Expropriation of
      Foreign Assets 40
  3.5 Downward Trend in Taking of Foreign Assets 41
  3.6 Conclusions 42

4 Negotiation of International Sales Contracts 46
- 4.1 Introduction 46
- 4.2 The Goods 46
- 4.3 Time of Delivery 47
- 4.4 Place of Delivery 48
- 4.5 The Payment Contract 48
- 4.6 A Brief Discussion of the Most Popular Types of Countertrade 52
- 4.7 Some Important Points to be Considered in Relation to Countertrade 55
- 4.8 Carriage of Goods (Transportation) Contract 56
- 4.9 Replacement and Service 56
- 4.10 Negotiation for the Sale of Second-hand/Used Products 57
- 4.11 Conclusions 57

5 Negotiation of Transfer of Technology Contracts 58
- 5.1 Introduction 58
- 5.2 The Important Elements of a Contract for the Transfer of Technology 59
- 5.3 Contents of the Contract 60
- 5.4 Conclusions 68

6 Project Finance 70
- 6.1 Introduction 70
- 6.2 Risks 72
- 6.3 Third Party Undertakings 73
- 6.4 Security for Payment 76
- 6.5 Inter-Lender Arrangements 80
- 6.6 Some General Issues that Should be Considered in Accepting a Property as Security 80
- 6.7 Registration of Securities 82
- 6.8 Some Important Legal Issues Pertaining to Project Finance 84
- 6.9 Conclusions 92

7 Negotiation of Syndicated Loan Agreements 96
- 7.1 Introduction 96
- 7.2 The Initiation of a Syndication 96
- 7.3 The Negotiation Process 97
- 7.4 Organisation of Syndicated Loans 99
- 7.5 The Lead Manager 100

7.6	The Agent	101
7.7	Offer and Acceptance of a Syndicated Loan	103
7.8	Some of the Most Important Clauses that are Included in Syndicated Loan Agreements	104
7.9	Conclusions	108

8 Negotiation of International Construction Contracts — 109
- 8.1 Introduction — 109
- 8.2 Preparation for Negotiation of an International Construction Contract — 110
- 8.3 How Should an Employer Select a Construction Contractor? — 111
- 8.4 Is There any Standard Form of International Construction Contract? — 113
- 8.5 Some of the Most Important Clauses in International Construction Contracts — 113
- 8.6 Conclusions — 130

9 Negotiation of Petroleum Contracts — 132
- 9.1 Introduction — 132
- 9.2 The Principal Features of State Contracts — 136
- 9.3 Principal Contractual Terms in a Petroleum Agreement — 138
- 9.4 Some General Comments on International Petroleum Contracts — 142
- 9.5 Conclusions — 144

10 The Role of the Lawyer in Negotiating International Commercial Contracts: Some Comments — 146
- 10.1 Introduction — 146
- 10.2 Jurisdictional Issues and Governing Law — 148
- 10.3 Conclusions — 149

Bibliography — 150
Index — 152

Table of Cases

AGIP and the Popular Republic of the Congo, 21 *International Legal Materials* (1982) 726.
Alcom Ltd. v. Republic of Colombia [1984] 2 All ER 6.
Asian Agricultural Products Ltd. and the Republic of Sri Lanka, 30 *International Legal Materials* (1991) 580.
Bacus Sri v. Sercio Nacional Del Trigo [1957] 1 QB 438.
Banco Creditor Agricol De Cartago, Barke v. Bancomer 762 F.2d.222 (2d Cir. 1985).
B.P. Exploration Co. (Libya) Ltd. v. Government of the Libyan Arab Republic (1979) 53 *International Law Reports* 297.
Birch Shipping Co. v. Republic of Tanzania, 507 F Supp. 311 (Ddc) 1980.
Callejo v. Bancomer 764 F.2d. (5th Cir. 1985).
Chile v. France (The Guano Case) *UN Report*, Vol. Xv, at 77.
Compania Mercantil Agrentina v. United States Shipping Board (1914) 131 Lt 388.
Eastern Timber Corporation v. Republic of Liberia, 659 F. Supp. 606 (DDC 1987).
Edward Owen Engineering Ltd. v. Barclays Bank International [1978] 1 All ER 976.
Factory at Charzow (Germany v. Poland) (1928) PCIJ, Series A, No. 17.
Government of the State of Kuwait and the American Independent Oil Co. (Aminoil), ICSID Arbitration, 21 *International Legal Materials* (1982) 976.
Gulf Bank v. Mitsubishi [1994] 2 LLR 149.
Hungarian P.R. v. Onori, 23 *International Law Reports* (1956) 203.
I Congress Del Partido [1981] 3 WLR 329.
Kleihs v. Republic of Austria, Ann, Digest (1948).
Krajina v. Tass Agency [1949] 2 All ER 274.
Liberia Eastern Timber Corporation v. Republic of Liberia, 659 F. Supp. 606 (DDC 1987).
Luther v. Sagor [1921] 3 KB 532.
Mobil Oil Iran Inc. and others v. Government of the Islamic Republic of Iran and National Iranian Oil Co., 86 *International Law Reports* (1991) 231.
National Oil Corporation (Libya) and the Libyan Sun Oil Co. (U.S.), 29 *International Legal Materials* (1990) 605.
Nuclear Tests Cases, *ICJ Reports* (1974) 253.
In Re Oil Spill by Amico Cadiz off the Coast of France, 16 March 1978.
The Schooner Exchange v. Mcfadden (1812) 7 Cranch 116.
SEDCO Inc. v. Iranian Oil Co. and the Islamic Republic of Iran, Iran–US Claims Tribunal, Awards of 24 October 1985, 27 March 1986 and 2 July 1987, 84 *International Law Reports* (1991) 484.

Storelli v. Governer Della Republic Francesse, Ann. Digest 2 (1923–4).
Sultan of Jahore v. Abubakar [1952] A.C. 318.
Texaco Overseas Petroleum Co. and California Asiatic Oil Co. v. the Government of the Libyan Republic (1979) 53 *International Law Reports* 389.
Trail Smelter Arbitration (1941) 3 RIAA 1905.
Trendtex Trading Corporation v. Central Bank of Nigeria [1977] QB 529.

Table of International Conventions and Resolutions

Brussels Convention on the Liability of Operators of Nuclear Ships, 1962.
Convention Establishing the Multilateral Investment Guarantee Agency, 1985.
Convention for the Prevention of Marine Pollution by Dumping from Ships and Aircraft, 1972.
Convention for the Prevention of Marine Pollution by Dumping of Wastes and Other Matter, 1972.
Convention for the Prevention of Marine Pollution from Land-based Sources, 1974.
Convention for the Protection of Birds Useful to Agriculture, 1902.
Convention for the Protection of the Ozone Layer, 1985.
Convention on Civil Liability for Oil Pollution Damage Resulting from Exploration and Exploitation of Seabed Mineral Resources, 1977.
Convention on the Control of Transboundary Movements of Hazardous Wastes and their Disposal, 1989.
Convention on the International Liability for Damage Caused by Space Objects, 1972.
Convention on the Regulation of Antarctic Mineral Resource Activities, 1988.
European Convention of State Immunity, 1972.
ILA Helsinki Rules on the Uses of the Waters of International Rivers, 1966.
International Convention on Civil Liability for Oil Production Damage, 1969.
International Convention on the Establishment of an International Fund for Compensation for Oil Pollution Damage, 1971.
International Convention for the Prevention of Pollution from Ships (MARPOL) 1973.
London Convention for the Prevention of the Pollution of the Sea by Oil, 1954.
London Convention Relative to the Preservation of Fauna and Flora in the Natural State, 1933.
Off-shore Pollution Liability Agreement, 1974.
Paris Convention on Third Party Liability in the Field of Nuclear Energy, 1960.
Peace Treaty with Italy, 1947, UNTS, Vol. 49, 126.
Principles Concerning Transfrontier Pollution (OECD), 1974.
Tanker Owners' Voluntary Agreement Concerning Liability for Oil Production (TOVALOP) 1969.
The Rio Declaration, 1992.The World Charter for Nature, 1982.
UN Code of Conduct on Transnational Corporations, 1992.
UN Convention on Long-range Transboundary Air Pollution, 1982.

UN General Assembly Resolution entitled 'The Charter of Economic Rights and Duties of States', 1974.
UN General Assembly Resolution on Permanent Sovereignty over Natural Resources, 1962.
Vienna Convention on Civil Liability for Nuclear Damage, 1962.
Vienna Convention on Succession of States in Respect of Treaties, 1978.
Warsaw Convention for the Unification of Certain Rules Relating to International Carriage by Air, 1929.

1 Some Basic Concepts Fundamental to Negotiation of International Commercial Contracts

1.1 Introduction

The negotiation of international commercial contracts requires certain techniques. The international commercial world seems to proceed on the presumed belief that businessmen are aware of such techniques and that experience matters most. It should be pointed out in this context that where a party enjoys monopoly on a market, the question of negotiating a contract would not arise, as the stronger party imposes its terms upon the weaker, but where competitors are available in a market, the technique of negotiating a contract assumes great importance, which is increasingly the case in the current international commercial world. Furthermore, there seems to exist a perception that the economically weaker world lacks bargaining power; consequently, the old-fashioned technique based on old-fashioned attitudes is often activated in negotiating international commercial contracts with such parties.

It is to be emphasised that in the current international commercial world choices exist, hence the need for learning the technique of negotiating international commercial contracts, irrespective of the economic and financial standing of the other party.

In this chapter an attempt is made to explain some of the concepts which are considered to be fundamental to negotiating an international commercial contract.

1.2 What is Negotiation?

To negotiate means to 'hold communication or conference for the purpose of arranging some matter by mutual agreement, to discuss a matter with a view to some settlement or compromise'.[1] To compromise means the settlement of a dispute by mutual concession.

As the definition indicates, to negotiate is to confer with others, with the object of reaching a compromise or an agreement. In this process, mutual concessions may have to be made. In other words, in a negotiation process, negotiators must not rigidly adhere to their own terms and conditions, as that will defeat the whole basis for and purpose of negotiation. Lack of flexibility on the part of a negotiating team would mean that the team wishes to hold the upper hand and to try to impose its terms and conditions on the other party. It is to be emphasised that in a negotiating process both parties' position must be treated as equal, and the terms and conditions that may be reached by mutual concession, will lead to a contract with a high probability of being performed.

1.3   Negotiation and Conflict

The meaning of the term 'negotiation' has already been explained. 'Conflict' means an encounter with arms, fight, battle, a prolonged struggle, the clashing or variance of opposed principles, statements or arguments.[2]

Based on this meaning, it is possible to maintain that conflict has no place in negotiation. In fact, the term should not be used to describe the hurdles that negotiators may experience in negotiating international commercial contracts. 'Differences of opinion' are different from 'conflict'. It is the very purpose of negotiation to iron out the differences between the parties by mutual concession. The perception of conflict in a negotiating process is not only irrelevant but also damaging; it may adversely affect the sense of mutuality in negotiation. The differences may quickly be resolved if parties come to negotiation with alternative proposals and strategies. Differences of opinion should be anticipated, otherwise there would be no need for negotiation. Differences of opinion arise as each party wants to gain as much as it can from a deal. The objective of negotiation is to reach a compromise by a process of narrowing down the differences and eventually agreeing on all issues for the purpose of concluding the contract.

1.4 What is not Negotiation

No intention to compromise with the other party is a symptom of a non-negotiating attitude. The attributes of negotiation are: flexibility, mutuality, compromise and non-aggressiveness. Absence of these attributes certainly confirms that there is no basis for negotiation. Negotiation sessions are often characterised by aggressiveness on the part of a party or domination by it, giving the impression that the other party must accept the terms of the domineering party. This is a mistake in that such impression or attitude is not only against the tenets of international commercial negotiation but also descriptive of the environment of negotiation, by provoking the other party to adopt an inflexible attitude, in consequence of which the negotiation process may break down.

Negotiation of political differences and negotiation of international commercial contracts are two different processes although both of them aim at agreements on mutually agreed terms. In international commercial negotiations there is no room for aggressiveness, domination, nor is there any room for emotion. International commercial negotiations are for settling business terms and conditions in relation to a deal which will be incorporated in a contract. Unlike diplomatic or political negotiations which are concerned with settlement of disputes or differences, international commercial negotiation is primarily concerned with determining the terms and conditions on the basis of which a particular commercial deal will be acted upon; the differences that may arise are based on the parties' perception of financial gains and losses.

Business on unilateral terms does not require any negotiation. It is important to emphasise that in a proper contract, two minds must meet, and negotiation is the process that brings this about.

1.5 The Environment of Negotiation

The environment of negotiation is created by the participants themselves. It is therefore essential that they do not act in a way that might damage the environment of negotiation. There are several factors that may contribute to a congenial environment of negotiation; friendly behaviour without giving any impression of superiority over the other party; a courteous manner; a flexible attitude towards the terms of negotiation; eagerness to negotiate rather than to impose one's own terms on the other; paying full attention to what the other party says and appreciating their difficulty or situation; respect for the host country's culture; ensuring that the foreign negotiators do not offend the host in any way.

Environment in this context stands for the environment that is created by the participants themselves and not the environment in the room in which negotiation takes place. A fully briefed negotiating team contributes to the environment by averting misunderstanding and confusion. Negotiation is similar to acting on a stage where success or failure may be assessed almost instantaneously. It is imperative that one team by its own behaviour does not antagonise the other team.

The team leaders have a significant role to play in maintaining a congenial environment for negotiation by settling differences between the teams amicably.

Cutting off a negotiation process is much easier than continuing with it. A continuation of the process is possible only if the environment is amicable. Aggressiveness, an assumption of superiority, misconceived ideas, ruthlessness or lack of manners simply destroy the environment of negotiation. The environment of negotiation therefore stands for an atmosphere that will enhance the process of negotiation, and the onus of creating and maintaining it is on the members of the teams and their leaders.

1.6 Interdependence and Negotiation

In order to understand the connection between interdependence and negotiation, one should refer to the definition of 'negotiation'. Mutuality is the cornerstone of negotiation. The assumption of superiority is derogatory to a negotiation process.

Negotiation should be based on the premises that without a buyer, a seller is unable to sell his product and *vice versa*. This point is particularly important when sellers are mere players on saturated markets. On the other hand, even in a seller's market, buyers should not be left with the impression of being dominated.

A good negotiator negotiates for the future also; that is, a negotiation should not be treated as a one-off affair. An understanding between a buyer and a seller offers the platform for future business. The issue of interdependence becomes extremely important when a buyer is required to obtain certain goods which are not easily available, and for the seller, when not too many buyers may be available.

A strong sense of interdependence becomes inevitable in a low market, whether caused by a general economic depression or by a general downward trend in the demand for a product.

The sense of interdependence should not lead to any surrender to the other party, it is best employed to create an atmosphere of friendliness, demonstrating eagerness to strike a deal, rather than becoming the source of negative attitudes.

When a negotiation fails, both parties lose. Negotiation should not be regarded merely as a gesture to arrange the conclusion of a contract; the arrangement must include the strategies and the identification of issues that will be discussed at negotiation sessions, which must be settled at the pre-negotiation session. A contract negotiation session is a session at which the terms must be discussed in a friendly fashion, with an understanding of interdependence.

1.7   Professionalism in Negotiation

Professionalism in negotiation is not only desirable but also a key to success. 'Professionalism' means 'the qualities or typical features of a profession'.[3] A 'profession' means a 'vocation or calling especially one that involves some branch of advanced learning'.[4] The technique of negotiating international commercial contracts is a technique which ought to be learned thoroughly; experience in it is not sufficient through understanding of the other party's goals and objectives, the business environment in the country of the other party, and even some knowledge of history and geography are essential.

Even where cultural differences between the parties and the language of negotiation may present certain difficulties, professionalism, which includes good manners and etiquette and the sense of interdependence may make up the deficiencies and maintain a friendly environment. There is therefore no point in becoming unnecessarily informal and/or using unprofessional or bad language. Manners, etiquette and appropriate language always contribute towards creating a good impression on the other party.

Members of a team should address the members of the other team correctly, and must also know the positions they hold. The mandate of each of the members in both teams must be known to all the members. Nothing must be mentioned about the cultural differences between the two countries, whether during or after the negotiation, as it would simply be derogatory to do so. Negotiation must take a neutral position, and it is an art to know how to remain neutral.

Socialising beyond certain limits can also create a bad impression of the professionalism of a person. A negotiating team should know the culture of a country and do things in conformity with it during their stay in that country. Awareness of such factors reflects directly upon professionalism, and each member of a negotiating team visiting a foreign country should be especially cognisant of them.

Professionalism in this context stands for two things: (a) professionalism of the team as a whole; and (by) professionalism of each member of the team. The leader of a negotiating team has therefore a special duty to make each member aware of this issue.

1.8 Conclusions

Having discussed the basic elements of negotiation, it would be appropriate to catalogue a few points in the form of 'do's' and 'don'ts' of negotiation techniques. This catalogue can never be a complete one. It simply itemises some of the most important points which a negotiator may find useful to remember in carrying out a successful negotiation.

Do's

(a) Consider any commercial negotiation in its long-term context.
(b) Prepare each negotiator's brief accurately.
(c) Each member of the negotiating team (negotiator) must know the background information relating to the proposed negotiation.
(d) Each team must know the requirements of the other team.
(e) Each team must know the socio-economic and legal environment of the other team.
(f) Must seek to succeed by co-operation.
(g) Must think of joint gains.
(h) Must trade something for something.
(i) Must break the link between winning and intimidation or domination.
(j) Must demonstrate professionalism.
(k) Must maintain a positive rather than a negative attitude.
(l) Must remain amiable in order to maintain a friendly environment of negotiation.
(m) Must avoid manipulative techniques.
(n) Must be tough when the other team is tough (but remain polite).

(o) Must remain firm, but not aggressive.
(p) Must ignore all threats by the other party.
(q) If the other party becomes aggressive or unreasonable, speak more quietly and slowly than they do, but be articulate.

Don'ts

(a) be submissive.
(b) be aggressive.
(c) be abusive.
(d) be intimidating.
(e) be domineering.
(f) be vague or ambiguous in respect of the terms and conditions of the proposed contract.
(g) be impolite.
(h) make personal attacks.
(i) comment adversely on national culture, including national business culture and history.
(j) socialise unduly.
(k) be rigid in negotiating terms and conditions, and do put forward alternative terms and conditions.
(l) comment on the political situation in the host country.
(m) be clumsy in dress and/or manners.
(n) make jokes which might offend the host or the guest as the case may be.
(o) use bad language.
(p) wrongly address any member of the team of the other party.
(q) prolong negotiation unnecessarily.
(r) personalise the negotiation process.
(s) defy the authority of the team leader.

Notes

1 *The Oxford English Dictionary*, Oxford, Clarendon Press (1989), vol. III p. 303.
2 Ibid., vol. III, p. 713.
3 *The Concise Oxford Dictionary*, Oxford, Clarendon Press (1990), p. 952.
4 Ibid.

2 Preparation for Negotiation

2.1 Introduction

The better the preparation, the higher are the chances of successfully conducting a negotiation, leading to the conclusion of a contract. At the preparation stage, each member of the team must consider his/her part of the job carefully, discussing between themselves difficult issues, and preparing strategies and alternative strategies.

Preparation of the subject matter of negotiation varies from project to project; nevertheless, there are certain elements which are common to most preparatory stages of contract negotiation.

The purpose of this chapter is to identify and illustrate some of the most common elements of negotiation which should receive attention at the pre-negotiation stage.

2.2 Elements Common to the Preparatory Stages of Negotiation

The preparatory stage cannot be activated unless the basic information about the proposed contract is at hand. In other words, both parties must have prepared the basic document in connection with the proposed contract negotiation.

In so far as the buyer is concerned, sometimes the publicity given by a prospective seller as to its product may provide the basic information to him. On the other hand, a buyer may already have some basic idea of what he wants to buy and can seek a product from a specific manufacturer or seller. In either case, the prospective buyer must have some background information which may give him a lead to the negotiation process, there is no point in going to a foreign jurisdiction without having some basic information on the product.

The basic information on the product must be examined and analysed by the prospective buyer to determine whether the product may serve his purpose; and if not, the extent to which the elements or features of the product may be altered and the probable expenses entailed, or whether an alternative product manufactured by the party may be considered. Where a prospective buyer knows his requirements, he should clearly state the specifications of the product in writing, and deliver them to the prospective manufacturer or seller. The pre-negotiation stage cannot start until the prospective manufacturer or seller has confirmed (preferably in writing) that he may be able to supply the specific product. This is an important factor in activating the preparatory stage for negotiation.

Ideally, through communications the parties should notify each other of the members of the negotiating team, including their names, positions within the organisation, in addition to the dates of arrival at and departure from the manufacturer's or seller's jurisdiction. The language of negotiation should be settled before departing for the foreign country and a translator taken with the team, where necessary.

The negotiating team of each party must consist of competent people, and their competence must be judged by reference to the product a buyer contemplates buying. In negotiating an engineering product, for example, an engineer qualified in the appropriate branch of engineering science must be included in the team, in addition to other relevant persons, namely, marketing manager, financial executive and a lawyer. The composition of a negotiating team depends upon the nature of product or service to be negotiated from, and the financial capacity of the firm; thus, no specific criteria for composing a negotiating team may be established.

However, each team must have a leader who is also a member of it. The person chosen as leader of the team need not be an expert, but should be an all-rounder and a person who commands the respect of the other members of the team. He/she should be a person who is amiable, good-tempered, reliable and a problem-solver. He/she should be a person who can diffuse a conflict, coordinate the activities of the members of his/her team, communicate to the leader of the other team without feeling strained, and keep the negotiating process going in a smooth and friendly fashion.

2.3 The Briefing Session

Briefing sessions are to be treated as integral parts of the preparatory stage of a negotiation. Each member of the team must be briefed on his/her part in the negotiation by the leader of the team. In other words, the entire matter for negotiation must be divided into parts for the purpose of allocating duties to each member of the team. This will allow each member to learn beforehand the nature of the role he/she is required to play at the actual negotiating session and to prepare his/her questions accordingly.

One of the most important reasons for holding pre-negotiation sessions is to ensure that each member of the team is fully familiar with the role he/she is required to play at the actual negotiation session(s) and to allow them sufficient time to familiarise themselves with the specific issues which have been allocated to them. Members of the team must be advised by the leader to prepare ancillary questions which may be required to be raised at the actual negotiation session. This also means that members of the team must be knowledgeable enough to raise ancillary questions with reference to certain statements made by the other party during a negotiation process.

It is extremely important that the team leader ensures that each member of the team is fully familiar with the produce equipment that the organisation wishes to sell or buy and the details of it, including the alternatives that the organisation may be prepared to consider. Identification of strategies and determination of the room for manoeuvre are two important issues that should be considered at the pre-negotiation stage. Strategies may be clearly identified provided the organisation possesses a clear idea of its requirements.

Identification of a clear idea as to the requirements of an organisation in terms of the product which it contemplates buying is one of the most important functions of the pre-negotiation stage. This argument is equally applicable to a seller, that is, a seller must also know his product thoroughly, and be ready with possible alternatives. This is where the team leader is required to take an important role. In order to identify the requirements of an organisation, he/she must have had clarification from higher authorities and a mandate as to the parameters of the negotiation.

It is elementary that briefing sessions should not be held until the team, including its members, has been approved of by the organisation, and the leader of the team has received a clear-cut mandate from the organisation. This point is also important for another reason – in the event of anything going wrong with the negotiation of the contract, the organisation may attempt to establish liability on the part of the team, and in particular, the team leader. Nothing should be done on an oral basis, as the legal consequences may be far-reaching. Internal memos, however unofficial, are enough to establish the parameters of a mandate given to a team, including its leader, by the organisation. A mandate is a crucially important document for the team leader and the team.

The purpose of the pre-negotiation stage is to ensure the following:

(a) that the team leader and the team have the requisite mandate to negotiate a contract;
(b) that each member of the team has been fully briefed as to his/her role;
(c) that the parameters of the mandate for negotiating a contract are identified;
(d) that the room for manoeuvre, if any, is determined;
(e) that the strategies of negotiation have been clearly identified;
(f) that alternative strategies have been identified and understood by each member of the team; and
(g) that the limits to negotiation have been identified.

2.4 The Stage Prior to Leaving for a Foreign Jurisdiction

At this stage, a team should familiarise itself with some of the basic aspects of the country which it is about to visit, such as the country's international commercial history, its culture and the business environment. A knowledge of the history of the country is necessary to understand the political and commercial relationship she has maintained with the country from which the team comes. A friendly relationship between the two countries should put the teams at ease, which should help create a friendly environment for the negotiation; this is a psychological factor, but it has great business impact. On the other hand, it is an important technique to learn how to revive or create a business relationship with a country with which in the recent past political relations have been strained or with which a new relationship is to be established. This second situation is much trickier than the first, but a negative or diffident attitude will not help. It is quite possible for a negotiator to re-establish rapport with a country with which there has been an unfriendly relationship in the recent past, or with which there has been no business relationship in the past at all.

A country's commercial history gives a prospective negotiating team a good account of the nature of the international commerce and business she has been engaged in, and the kinds of goods and industry in which she has dealt. It is also worth knowing the country's infrastructure, and such basic information as the nature of the import-export trade pattern, balance of payments position, structure of the economy etc. This issue has been detailed in the next chapter under the heading 'feasibility study'.

A negotiating team should also be familiar with the industrial, economic and monetary policies of a country, and in particular, her external debt position. Furthermore, the strengths of the country in the various sectors of the economy should be identified.

Prior to their leaving for the foreign jurisdiction, the members of the team should be required to familiarise themselves with the culture of the foreign jurisdiction, in addition to knowing the legal and economic environment. There cannot be anything more disastrous than to comment adversely on the host country. It simply spoils the negotiation process. It is well worth learning a few simple things about the culture of the foreign country, and trying not to do anything contrary to that country's culture.

2.5 Eligibility for Membership of a Negotiating Team

A negotiating team must be open-minded, and fully prepared to listen to the other party's strategies, rather than imposing its own ideas and terms upon them. Mutuality is the basic key to a successful negotiation. The preparatory stage must cater for such training and orientation of the members of the negotiating team. The sense of interdependence must be developed during this stage too.

In selecting members of the team, attention should be paid by the team leader to choosing those people who have the tenacity and broad-mindedness to learn about and the ability to cope with a foreign culture and business environment. Many people may not possess these qualities. If the other party has reason to hold superior bargaining power, the team should be made aware of that, and should prepare its strategies accordingly. In selecting its members, the team leader should consider very seriously that it is not only the experience of an employee that matters but also the qualities mentioned above. It is important to bear in mind that the scenario of international contract negotiations is constantly changing.

2.6 Conclusions

Preparation for negotiation is more important than the actual stage of negotiation in that the briefing of members of a team is crucial for successfully concluding a deal. The preparation stage cannot be successful in the absence of suitable team members. Two objectives are important at this stage: (a) to make the strategies absolutely clear; and (b) to ensure that every member of the team has understood them. The loyalty of the members to the leader of the team must also be ensured. The qualities that a member should posses have already been identified. It is not a question of satisfying these criteria and qualities on paper; the genuine feeling that each member can satisfy them is important. A team leader has thus an enormous responsibility in selecting the members of his/her team.

3 Negotiation of International Commercial Contracts and Risks

3.1 Introduction

In negotiating any international contract the probable risks that might frustrate its performance must be considered. Risks may relate to the country in which the contract would be performed or they may relate to the subject matter of the contract or both. One of the means of determining risks is to develop a feasibility study, which may be prepared by sellers or investors themselves, or by experts who are available to prepare such studies.

This chapter deals with two primary matters: (a) feasibility studies; and (b) the types of risk a party may be required to consider in negotiating an international contract.

3.2 Feasibility Studies

A feasibility study stands for a study of the practicability of a proposed project. In order to determine the practicability of a project, information on different relevant matters is necessary, such as the sources of finance, potential of the project, availability of materials and equipment, existing manpower and projected manpower, export potential of the finished product where relevant, logistics, climatic conditions, the political situation and the foreign debts accrued by the country.

It is not possible to itemise all the matters which should be considered in preparing a feasibility study, the development of which depends upon the nature of the proposed project. The feasibility study for setting up a school, for example, and that for an international construction contract will be different, although certain common issues may have to be considered in relation to all feasibility studies.

Feasibility studies should be prepared by experts having knowledge and experience of similar kinds of project. A feasibility study is the blueprint of a project. The higher the quality of a feasibility study, the better is the prospect of correctly evaluating a proposed project. A feasibility study will also reveal the probable risks involved in pursuing a proposed project. Similarly, a feasibility study will allow an investor to consider the kind of precautionary measures it ought to take against probable risks.

The usefulness of a feasibility study depends upon the kind of information it has relied upon. It is therefore very important that the sources of information relied upon in developing a feasibility study are of a primary nature. Information on country profiles may be obtained from various sources, such as government departments and various international and intergovernmental and non-governmental institutions. Of course, in many countries genuine and reliable information on various issues may not be available as they do not have a system of maintaining them. Relevant organisations, international, intergovernmental with governmental and non-governmental, may provide some information on almost every country in the world. Lack of information on a country or a project simply increases the incidence of risks; consequently, investors sometimes become overcautious about investing in foreign jurisdictions. Host countries should take the initiative to provide as much information as possible on a proposed project, when requested by a proposed investor.

In order to be able to attract foreign investors, host countries should genuinely attempt to establish the projected export earnings from the proposed investment, and whether after completion of the programme, the host country would be able to operate the project with the help of local people, although arrangements for supervision by the foreign investor may have to be made for some time.

The country's balance of payments, and balance of trade position, together with the exchange control regulations where relevance must be taken into account in preparing a feasibility study. The provision for training of local people and the opportunities for maintaining a flow of competent people to operate the project should be clearly identified in a feasibility study.

A feasibility study is not *per se* a legally binding document, but if a host country gives a warranty as to the authenticity of the information provided by her in the preparation of a feasibility study, it will have legal effect; hence the need for providing correct and genuine information.

Most of the international organisations, such as the International Bank for Reconstruction and Development or the International Monetary Fund, have their own method of developing feasibility studies on programmes on which loans are sought by their Member States; however in seeking loans from other sources, such as syndications, the applicant should develop its own feasibility study so as to provide a comprehensive picture of the project.

3.3 A Brief Analysis of Some of the Usual Risks Associated with Private Foreign Investments

Risks may be broadly divided into two categories: pre-completion and post-completion risks. Depending upon the nature of a project, the type and magnitude of risks vary. The general types of risk which are relevant to most projects have received attention in this Section.

3.3.1 Political Risks

Political risks constitute a significant part of the entire domain of risks. These risks may take different forms: instability of a government; passing of new legislation giving insufficient or no notice to foreign investors or a total change of the investment policy in a particular sector of the economy; or the taking (nationalisation/expropriation) of foreign assets in the national interest. Although such risks are foreseeable, protective measures may not always be available. In the West however, most of the governments offer insurance policies against such risks. In the United Kingdom, ECGD (Export Credit Guarantee Department) policies or in the United States, the policies issued by OPIC (Overseas Private Investment Corporation), offer financial remedies to their national investors when they invest abroad, although in most cases, the total investment is not covered by such policies.

For over a decade, the Multilateral Investment Guarantee Agency (MIGA), established under the auspices of the World Bank have formed insurance policies to private foreign investors if they are prepared to invest in the developing world, provided of course certain conditions are satisfied, but these policies exclude 'non-discriminatory measures of a general application which governments normally take for the purpose of regulating economic activity in their territories', although they may cover risks relating to:

> Expropriation and similar measures (including legislative or administrative action) which will have the effect of depriving the holder of a guarantee of his ownership or control or a substantial benefit from the investment.

One is required to accept that every sovereign power in the world has the inherent right to take assets of national or foreigners in the national interest, but in the event of the taking of assets of foreigners, customary international law requires states to pay the owners of assets compensation. It would be appropriate to point out in this connection that the incidence of political risks which gained momentum during the core decolonisation period (1960–80) have now significantly decreased.

3.3.2 Currency and Transfer Risks

Fluctuations in currency value give rise to currency risks. Precautionary measures may be taken against such risks, either by fixing the currency exchange rate, or by hedging.

Transfer risks arise when a government prohibits by regulatory measures the transfer of profits, royalties etc. in hard currencies from its own jurisdiction to the relevant foreign jurisdiction. Of course this risk no longer exists within the European Union. Protection against transfer risks is often taken by seeking warranties from the governments concerned whereby transfer of payments or royalties is secured by foreign investors.

3.3.3 Credit Risks

The nature of the financial standing of a participant helps determine the nature of credit risks, a country's balance of payments and balance of trade position will certainly give a clear idea as to the prospect of a government party meeting its commitments. The current debt situation and the record of servicing of loans are important factors to determine this risk. A country's position with international financial organisations should offer useful information on the credit rating of the country. The available capability of the country to operate the project whether immediately after its completion, or within the foreseeable future, should be considered in determining credit risks. Whether a country is often a victim of calamity risks is an issue that should not be disregarded in determining the credit risks, as priority must be accorded to such emergencies by the government prior to its meeting its international obligations.

The viability of the project and the prospect of making it profit-earning should receive the attention of the negotiating parties in determining the extent of this risk. The caution must be entered that if credit risks are not appropriately evaluated, the risk can be two-dimensional: first, an investor may venture on an unprofitable and risky investment; second, many profitable investments may be thrown away. One should not evaluate this risk on the basis of any preconceived ideas. Guarantees may be sought against credit risk. Whether the other party is a government or a private body, guarantees are usually sought from banks.

In the case of the other party being a private body, the profit and loss account of the party for the previous three years or so may give a general idea of the performance of the party. It will also give a clear idea of its debt situation and its record of servicing loans. As in the case of a government, the capability of the party, in terms of technical knowledge, management etc. should also be looked into.

Credit risks may be secured by including 'performance requirements' in a contract, and the provision of 'buy back' (whereby the foreign manufacturer will be required to buy a percentage of its own product in a designated hard currency) may alleviate this risk.

3.3.4 Operational Risks

Operational risks may be caused by internal and external factors: internal factors are those factors which are caused by internal causes, namely, lock-out, strikes or other forms of labour dispute, interruption in the supply of essential goods and materials etc. Export prohibition or prohibition of travel by experts imposed by the government of the manufacturer's or investor's country, are examples of external factors. Any risk that may interrupt the operation of a project may be described as an operational risk. At the negotiation stage, parties should agree to alternative sources of supply and incorporate the agreed alternative sources of supply into the contract. In practice, however, in the event of the operation of a project being suspended for the lack of supply of materials, both parties wait for a reasonable period of time to see whether the situation changes or not. Contingency plans should therefore be discussed at the negotiation stage, and the cost implications thereof. This point has been further developed under the title 'expert dependency risk'.

Operational risks have a bearing upon the completion of a project. If delay in completing the project is occasioned by the default or inaction of the host country or the industry concerned in the host country, compensation may be claimed on the ground of a breach of contract. Many countries in the West cover such risks by means of insurance policies. In the event of operational risks continuing for a long period of time, parties usually agree not to proceed with the contract and in such a situation, they agree to accept the losses, although of course, in most cases such losses are recovered by activating insurance policies. The caution must be entered that in the event of operational risks being occasioned by any party to the contract, no benefit from any insurance policy may be derived.

Where operational risks are seasonal, contract negotiation should take that point into consideration, and work schedules should be prepared accordingly. In many countries, draught or rainy season often hampers constructional or other similar types of work. It is for negotiators to take precautionary measures against such risks.

3.3.5 Smooth Running of the Project Risks

Whereas operational risks may be described as pre-completion risks, the smooth running of the project is a post-completion risk. Again, such risks may be occasioned by internal or external factors. If the smooth running of a project is hindered by the lack of supply of materials or labour by the local party, then it is occasioned by internal factors; lack or stoppage of supply of materials or experts from the foreign party or absence of maintenance of the project by the foreign party may equally hinder the smooth running of a project or any lack of trained personnel. This last form of risk may be avoided by introducing a training programme, through a turn-key contract, which is often concluded as an integral part of the project agreement.

Both operational risks and the smooth running of the project risk may be occasioned by deteriorating political relations between the home and host countries. In such a situation, the *force majeure* clause should not be activated immediately to bring the contract to an abrupt end. At the negotiation stage, alternative means of protecting the project or its smooth running should be considered and the agreed formula should be incorporated into the contract.

The smooth running of a project may also be hindered by construction problems or by the breakdown of machinery or other similar factors. Negotiators should consider these issues at the negotiation stage, and agree alternative means of running the project or provide for remedies in the contract.

Where smooth running of the project is hindered for an indefinite period of time and the prospect of resuming operational functions is remote, there is little point in the foreign investor staying in the host country. In such circumstances, the foreign investor may negotiate compensation with the host country or the industry in the country, as a case of abandonment. The proviso must be entered that the foreign investor did not contribute to causing the situation, as otherwise it may be treated as a case of breach of contract.

If smooth running of the project proves to be impossible owing to unforeseeable reasons, then abandonment becomes inevitable, and the foreign investor may seek remedies from the insurance company. It is therefore essential for foreign investors to look for comprehensive insurance policies, and to examine the nature of the cover they may be entitled to.

For smooth running of a project, host countries should try to rely upon local material and labour force, including experts as much as possible. Of course, during strikes and lock-outs, a party may encounter difficulties in providing an efficient and competent labour force. An investor should investigate whether experts and a similar labour force may be made available by a host country from a neighbouring component state (in the case of a federal state) or even a neighbouring country, at comparable cost, and provision for meeting such emergencies should be made by the parties at the negotiation stage.

3.3.6 Production and Sales Risk

These two risks may be considered together. Production risk stands for the failure to meet the production target; consequently, parties should provide for performance requirements in their contract. This is a risk which may be encountered after the completion of the project. The foreign company should be required to undertake the obligation of producing or manufacturing the product up to a target level; however in order to protect its position, the foreign company must also require the host party to undertake the obligation of providing materials and labour if so agreed. Where the supply of materials and labour is to be provided by a foreign party, production risk becomes a serious issue. Usually, it is for the foreign party to ensure that there will not be any difficulty in obtaining supply of materials from their chosen jurisdiction. This issue has been further discussed in a separate section of this work.

Where the failure to achieve the agreed level of production causes the host party to sustain losses, the latter can claim for damages, and provision to that effect should be made in the contract. Similarly, when production is hampered by the failure of the host party for whatever reason, the foreign party can claim for damages and disown liability, on the ground of a breach of contract. This issue assumes particular importance when the foreign party undertakes to 'buy back' a percentage of the product. In order to maintain production income at agreed levels, a 'due diligence' warranty from both parties is required. Another aspect of this issue has been discussed in this work under *force majeure*.

Sales risk may be caused by loss of production or slump in sales occasioned by lack of demand for the product. The issues relating to loss of production have already been discussed. In order to maintain a profit-earning sales level, the parties at the negotiation stage should discuss the channels of distribution of the product, and the division of duties in promoting sales, whether through publicity or advertising, or through public relations activity. Where a foreign subsidiary is engaged in the production work, the host party must also ascertain whose duty it would be to organise publicity and advertising and in what form. In many cases, if the same brand of product is manufactured by a subsidiary of a headquarter's company, the advertising and publicity work is usually undertaken by the foreign subsidiary so as to ensure that the brand-name related publicity is similar, if not identical, to that promoted by the headquarter's company. On the other hand, if the host party undertakes this work, clear provision should be made in the contract to that effect. It should also be clarified whether the text and design of each item of publicity and advertisement must be approved by the foreign party. The cost of publicity and advertisement is another issue, which should be clarified at the negotiation stage.

Sales risk may be caused by two other main factors: noncompetitive pricing and failure to meet the choice of buyers. It is elementary that a good marketing survey is a prerequisite for reaching any decision on this issue. It is primarily for the foreign party to undertake this responsibility, although the host party may be required to cooperate with the former in this regard.

Where a product is to be sold in both domestic and foreign markets, the strategies of sales may be different, and they should be clearly identified at the negotiation stage. Cultural differences and differences in taste may require a product to be manufactured differently as well as packaged differently. Sales of a product in the foreign manufacturer's domestic market are usually the responsibility of the foreign party. A condition of a 'guaranteed level of sales' is a harsh condition, although a provision may be made in the contract for an approximate level of sales. In the event of a failure to meet that level for consecutive periods (months or quarters), parties should be prepared to review the position, rather than initiating any breach of the contract. Transportation of the product including costs of transportation to the foreign market(s) is the responsibility of the foreign party.

Overproduction is a risk which should be avoided. It is a self-induced risk, and there can be no protection against this risk. Overproduction entails preservation and warehousing costs. It also depletes resources rapidly.

At the point of negotiation, the host party should point out whether the foreign party would encounter any export restrictions in respect of the product from the local government. Similarly, the host party should enquire of the foreign party the foreign markets it would like to explore, as often governments impose prohibitions on the exportation of products to certain foreign markets. In this connection parties should ensure that they do not violate any sanctions imposed by the United Nations.

3.3.7 Environmental Risks

Depending upon the nature of the project the parties undertake, precautionary measures against this risk should be taken. In respect of construction and mining projects, for example, it would be advisable for parties to obtain expert reports on this issue, which should clearly identify the nature of risks, if any, during the pre-completion and operational periods. In fact, in respect of most projects, the issue of environmental risks has assumed importance, and the growing awareness of the international community of these risks now requires foreign investors and host parties to pay serious attention to this issue.

Environmental risks may be caused by various factors: use of inappropriate technology; negligent use of technology; overuse of chemicals or toxic substances; emission of fumes or toxic substances etc. Either party may be responsible for it; therefore, the division of work, and the impact of it on the environment should be fully discussed by the parties at the negotiation stage.

One of the important features of environmental risk is that an underdeveloped economy or infrastructure may not be a sustainable excuse, as it falls on the foreign investor to ensure that its activities do not in any way pollute the environment. On the other hand, the host party must also ensure that it does not contribute in any way to environmental pollution.

A foreign investor should therefore ascertain the situation prior to its making any commitment to investment. The Rio Declaration of 1992,[1] which received support from the majority of the developing states, provides for very extensive obligations for a polluter. It would be advisable for all foreign investors to bear this issue in mind prior to their determining the kind of equipment or technology they may use in connection with their investment projects.

A host party may seek an enforceable guarantee from the foreign investor against such risks; on the other hand, in order to secure its position, the foreign investor may also like to seek such a guarantee from the host party. In any event, the clean-up process is extremely expensive, and it is not certain whether insurance companies may be able to offer insurance policies covering such risks.

It is to be appreciated that environmental risks are 'continuing risks' in that even after the completion of the project, these risks subsist during the operational period. One of the means of avoiding or minimising the incidence of these risks would be to make provision for periodic supervision by experts, or by the headquarter's company, and amend the position, if necessary.

Environmental risks are not confined to developing countries; they may be equally important issues for investment in the rich world. At the negotiation stage both parties should make their respective positions clear, and identify the bases for liability.

Jurisdictional issues assume particular importance in respect of environmental risks. The argument that a subsidiary is a mere agent of the parent company, and therefore a subsidiary's act is virtually to be regarded as an act of the parent company which controls the subsidiary, and as such the jurisdiction in which the parent company is located is the proper jurisdiction, may not be sustainable. In such case, the location in which the negligent act has caused damage or injury, whether to the economy or the people or both, will assume jurisdiction. In this connection one may like to consult the *Union Carbide* case.[2] It is therefore important that a foreign investor which usually operates as a subsidiary of a parent company takes precautionary measures in order to ensure that environmental risks are either minimised or that sufficient precautionary measures have been taken against these risks occurring, or that sufficient provision has been made for remedial measures, whether through insurance policies or otherwise.

By the same token, it may be stated that the law of the country in which the risk has taken place will be the law to determine the liability and damages. Protection of the environment has also become a focal point in public international law. In fact, issues relating to environmental risks are where relevant dealt with by referring to the principle of state responsibility. Identifiable principles of public international law are available to deal with environmental issues, and they are applied even though the cause of action may arise under a state contract.

The 'polluter pays' principle may operate as a deterrent to investment by transnational corporations, and many insurance companies may not be willing to undertake the high financial risks entailed in issuing insurance policies covering such risks. This is an area which requires the urgent attention of the insurance world and the world of science.

In so far as the developing countries are concerned, much attention should be paid to developing indigenous technology which would suit their own environment, irrespective of whether it is the most modern technology or not.

In the agriculture and light industry sectors it is possible to increase productivity by employing indigenous technology, which would not be environmentally unfriendly. As scientific expertise develops and the developing countries' capability increases, more technological sophistication may be achieved. Environmental education in both rich and poor countries seems to be an essential ingredient in protecting the environment from pollution. But, of course, where employment of high technology is essential, whether in the rich or poor world, for example in the extraction industry, precautionary measures are essential to ensure that the environment is not unduly polluted through lack of care and skill.

Environmental risk is a risk which cannot be dealt with overnight; it may be possible to take precautionary measures against the foreseeable aspects of the risk, until the full dimension of this risk has been ascertained.

As stresses on the environment have become increasingly pronounced, considerable attention has been directed over the last three decades to identify their causes, evaluate their long-term consequences and develop preventative and protective strategies. Although some progress in this regard has been achieved, the full impact of environmental damage still remains unexplored.

Furthermore, there does not seem to exist any universally accepted definition of environmental damage, although the issue of environmental damage has become a principal concern for investors. These problems are further compounded by the fact that a clean start is not possible; in many countries the environment is already polluted, and any further industrial activity will simply aggravate the pollution process. Given this situation, insurance companies also experience a dilemma as to what protection may be offered by them. However, over the last three decades or so (since the Stockholm Declaration of 1972), a growing awareness of environmental damage has become evident, and investors are required to pay sufficient attention to this issue in negotiating contracts.

In addition to discussing the growth and development of environmental awareness, and the impact of the 'polluter pays' principle, this section explains that in the absence of any specific rules of law at a national level, customary rules of international law pertaining to state responsibility and negligence are sufficient to deal with the issues of environmental liability.

3.3.8 What is Meant by Environmental Damage?

'Damage' according to the Concise Oxford dictionary, means 'harm or injury impairing the value or usefulness of something'. If this meaning of 'damage' is related to the environment, a general idea of what 'environmental damage' stands for may be ascertained. However, the problem remains that value judgement to a degree is entailed in determining environmental damage. 'Impairing the value or usefulness of something' is a phrase which accommodates such value judgement. Realistically, in determining the extent of damage allegedly caused by an investor, the claimant usually includes claims which are to a certain extent based on its value judgement; this becomes particularly evident in making claims on what would have been the profit or benefit over a determined future period or the potential of an individual had no injury been caused to him/her by pollutants or/by other industrial mishaps. Generally speaking, environmental damage stands for activities that damage the environment, that is, the soundness or purity of the environment.

The term 'environment' means 'physical surroundings and conditions, especially as affecting people's lives; conditions or circumstances of living external conditions affecting the growth of plants and animals', the latter pertaining to ecology. This definition of the 'environment' is extremely extensive, and any activity of an investor may be alleged to have come under this definition. If this definition is followed then it is not difficult to imagine the extent of risks an investor may undertake in pursuing its investment programmes.

This definition of the 'environment' requires investors to take preventative measures, by ensuring that no claim can be brought against them on the ground of the lack of 'duty of care and skills'. A degree of foreseeability as to what might cause injury is also necessary, including the use of technology, ingredients in manufacturing products, and the general impact on ecology, etc. The extensive nature of the definition of the term 'environment' enlarges the scope of risks for investors, hence the requirement for their taking precautionary measures.

There also remains the issue of taking 'curative measures', which is popularly described as the 'polluter pays' principle. This issue has been explained in a subsequent section of this work. Thus the range of the measures that an investor is required to take in regard to the broad issue of 'environmental damage' is enormous. On the other hand, no investor may disregard the issue of 'environmental risk'. Below is a list of the items that usually cause destructive effect on the environment and this list is by no means an exhaustive one.

- Pollution and toxification of air, water and soil;
- Degradation of land (deforestation, desertification etc.);
- Acidification of land based and water based ecosystems;

- Destruction of the stratospheric ozone layer; and
- Greenhouse gas-induced climatic change.

The effect may be felt on human beings and ecosystems. Any of the effects may be contributed to by the use of inappropriate technology, inappropriate chemicals, lack of appropriate policies and strategies by the investor, or even by failure to ascertain the existing degree of pollution, etc.

Certain types of energy are also likely to cause risks to human health or the environment.[3] In other words, sufficient precautionary and preventative measures must be taken by hazardous industries. 'Exportation of pollution' is a problem which arises from the transfer of environmentally harmful activities, installations or products prohibited or regulated by one country, into another. Industrial accidents and failure to adopt effective safety procedures are part of environmental damage.[4] Release of gaseous, liquid and solid wastes contributes to the environmental damage process. Furthermore, any contributory act, such as exportation of wastes to countries in which the laws are apparently lenient, may be regarded as a negligent act. Release of waste even within the jurisdiction of the home country, for example, chemical waste released in a river, which contaminates the water in the rivers across national boundaries, may be regarded as an act contributory to transnational environmental damage.

Pollution causes damage. According to the Organisation for European Co-operation and Development (OECD), 'pollution' means:

> ... the introduction by man, directly or indirectly, of substances or energy into the environment resulting in deleterious effects of such nature as to endanger human health, harm living resources and ecosystems, and impair or interfere with amenities and other legitimate uses of the environment.[5]

This definition is sufficiently extensive to include all types of pollution, marine, land-based or otherwise. Human activity whether direct or indirect contributes to most causes of environmental pollution and environmental damage. The impact of environmental damage is not uniform on human beings, animals, and ecosystems.

The causes of environmental damage are numerous, and so are its contributory factors. The effect of environmental damage may be far-reaching and perniciously costly. The determination of the damage is to a certain extent based on value judgement, although the principles applied for this purpose are well-recognised. Scientific research is certain to explore more causes of environmental damage in the future, and the 'polluter pays' principle is gaining ground. The extent of environmental risks is also increasing, as is the need for taking precautionary and preventative measures. Negotiators of international contracts cannot possibly disregard environmental risks, and therefore, it is essential that they are familiar with these risks.

Why negotiators may not disregard the issue of environmental risks The right to a healthy environment derives from the common interest of humanity, and the nexus between human rights and environmental protection is clearly established by Principle 1 of the Stockholm Declaration of 1972: 'Man has the fundamental right to freedom, equality and adequate conditions of life, in an environment of a quality that permits a life of dignity and well-being ...'. Since the Stockholm Declaration, the action of the international community for promoting the awareness required for the protection and preservation of the environment, in all its dimensions, has been consistent. The protection of the environment is considered not only as a part of human rights but also an integral factor for sustainable development, irrespective of the economic structure and the level of development of a country. Below is a list of some of the important Conventions and instruments that have been concluded for the protection and preservation of the environment generally, and certain specific aspects of the environment in particular.

- Convention for the Protection of Birds Useful to Agriculture, 1902;
- London Convention Relative to the Preservation of Fauna and Flora in their Natural State, 1933;
- London Convention for the Prevention of the Pollution of the Sea by Oil, 1954;
- Paris Convention on Third Party Liability in the Field of Nuclear Energy, 1960;
- Brussels Convention on the Liability of Operators of Nuclear Ships, 1962;
- Vienna Convention on Civil Liability for Nuclear Damage, 1962;
- ILA Helsinki Rules on the Uses of the Waters of International Rivers, 1966;
- Tanker Owners' Voluntary Agreement Concerning Liability for Oil Production (TOVALOP), 1969;
- International Convention on Civil Liability for Oil Production Damage, 1969;

28 *Negotiating Techniques in International Commercial Contracts*

- International Convention on the Establishment of an International Fund for Compensation for Oil Pollution Damage, 1971;
- Convention on the International Liability for Damage Caused by Space Objects, 1972;
- Convention for the Prevention of Marine Pollution by Dumping from Ships and Aircraft, 1972;
- Convention on the Prevention of Marine Pollution by Dumping of Wastes and Other Matter, 1972;
- International Convention for the Prevention of Pollution From Ships (MARPOL), 1973;
- Convention for the Prevention of Marine Pollution from Land-based Sources, 1974;
- Off-shore Pollution Liability Agreement, 1974;
- Convention on Civil Liability for Oil Pollution Damage Resulting from Exploration and Exploitation of Seabed Mineral Resources, 1977;
- UN Convention on Long-Range Transboundary Air Pollution, 1979;
- UN Convention on the Law of the Sea, 1982;
- The World Charter for Nature, 1982;
- Convention for the Protection of the Ozone Layer, 1985;
- Convention on the Regulation of Antarctic Mineral Resource Activities, 1988;
- Convention on the Control of Transboundary Movements of Hazardous Wastes and Their Disposal, 1989;
- The Rio Declaration on Environment and Development, 1992.

This is by no means an exhaustive list of the international Conventions. The Provisions of some of the Conventions mentioned above have also been by Protocols. In addition to the international Conventions there also exist many regional Conventions to protect the environment regionally. One of the most recent international attempts to develop international awareness in this field is the Rio Declaration of 1992.

These Conventions and other relevant instruments combined with the decisions of courts and tribunals are sufficient to establish that international awareness of the need for the protection and preservation of the environment has become manifest. The aspirations of the international community in this regard have become evident particularly in the Rio Declaration of 1992. When a country has adopted legislation to enforce a Convention, whether international or regional then negotiators must look into that legislation, in addition to other legislation that may be operational in that jurisdiction.

Negotiators must therefore be conversant with the customary rules of international law in regard to the protection and preservation of the environment which are usually developed by international Conventions, generally accepted resolutions of UN bodies, judicial decisions of courts and tribunals, particularly of an international standing, in addition to familiarising themselves with regional Conventions, if any, and the legislation operational in the jurisdiction concerned.

3.3.9 The European Union Position

Neither the EEC treaty nor the European Convention on Human Rights contains any statement of a fundamental or human right to a healthy environment. Although the first Community Directives pertaining to the issue of the protection of the environment were issued in the 1960s, it was not until 1972 at the Paris Conference that Heads of States made a specific declaration on the issue of the protection and preservation of the environment which stated that: '... particular attention will be given to intangible values and to protecting the environment, so that progress may really be part at the service of mankind'.[6] Without going into details, it may be pointed out that the European Conventions in subsequent years adopted various programmes of action for the protection and preservation of the environment. In Cases 240/831[7] and 302/862[8] the European Court confirmed that the protection of the environment must be regarded as an objective which is in the general interest of the Community. Title XVI of the Treaty on European Union, 1992 (the Maastricht Treaty) is devoted to Environment. Article 130r of the Treaty provides, inter alia, that:

> Community policy on the environment shall contribute to pursuit of the following objectives:
>
> − Preserving, protecting and improving the quality of the environment;
> − Protecting human health;
> − Prudent and rational utilisation of natural resources;
> − Promoting measures at international level to deal with regional or worldwide environmental problems.

Paragraph 3 of the same article provides that:

> In preparing its policy on the environment, the Community shall take account of:

- available scientific and technical data;
- environmental conditions in the various regions of the Community;
- the potential benefits and costs of action or lack of action;
- the economic and social development of the Community as a whole and the balanced development of its regions.

Article 130r(2) states that: 'Environmental protection requirements must be integrated into the definition and implementation of other Community policies'. This certainly clarifies the Community's commitment to protecting, preserving and improving the environment. The provisions of Title XVI must be read with other relevant provisions in the Treaty Establishing the Community, for example, the provisions as to harmonisation of laws. Article 103t of the Maastricht Treaty provides that:

> The protective measures adopted pursuant to Article 130s shall not prevent any Member State from maintaining or introducing more stringent protective measures. Such measures must be compatible with this Treaty...

If any conflict should arise between the provisions of the Treaty and a particular rule of law in a Member State, it may be resolved by relying upon the principles laid down by the European Court in Case 240/83 according to which the Community provisions will prevail even over the fundamental rights recognised by the Member States, provided the principle of proportionality and the rule against discrimination are reviewed. The principles established by the Court in Case 240/83 were reaffirmed by it in case 302/86.

It is not possible nor would it be appropriate to list out all important Recommendations, Directives and Resolutions adopted by the Community institutions in regard to the issue of the protection, preservation and improvement of the environment.

Suffice to say that the Community has, particularly since the 1970s, consistently developed principles and policies, albeit in a piecemeal fashion, until the Maastricht Treaty was concluded.[9] Under the EEC Treaty, as amended by the Single European Act, 1987, it is possible for an individual to bring actions before the European Court in relation to environmental matters (see Articles 164–188 and in particular Articles 173(2) and 175(2)). A particular procedure has also been developed for this purpose.

Negotiators should familiarise themselves with the EU policies and rules in regard to the protection, prevention and improvement of the environment prior to their negotiating any contract with a Member State of the European Union, in addition to studying the particular legislation that may be operational in that state. The guidelines developed by the Organisation for European Co-operation and Development (OECD) are also instructive in understanding this subject. These guidelines should be taken into consideration when negotiation is initiated with a developed country as all developed countries belong to this organisation.

3.3.10 The 'Polluter Pays' Principle

The 'polluter pays' principle was principally developed in the 1970s, in particular at the 1972 Stockholm Declaration, and thereafter reinforced by the 1992 Rio Declaration. This principle appeared also in the Guiding Principles concerning International Economic aspects of Environmental Policies adopted by the OECD.[10] It has provoked considerable controversy among investors.

One issue is whether third parties who may not be directly involved in the process of production should also bear the cost. This issue may be dealt with by ascertaining the degree of involvement of the third party and by determining the causal connection between the third party's involvement and the damage caused. The determination of the costs of the environmental damage is also another issue which must be considered under the 'polluter pays' principle. There is yet another controversy as to whether the cost of clean-up should be externalised or be borne by the polluter without any subsidy from any source. In the application of the 'polluter pays' principle to accidental pollution[11] the OECD indicated that insurance policies may be adopted to accommodate this principle; but of course, therein lies the problem – whether without knowing the full extent of environmental damage, an insurance policy may cover all risks.

The 'polluter pays' principle is well-recognised by the international community, and it would be rather difficult for investors to avoid its application in any country, be it a rich or a poor country. Again, in 1974, the OECD adopted principles concerning transfrontier pollution,[12] the primary objective of which is to initiate action with a view to preventing and controlling transfrontier pollution. It is evident that the polluter pays principle is extremely burdensome for transnational corporations. The UN Convention on Long-range Transboundary Air Pollution is another landmark in this respect. The 'polluter pays' principle should be regarded as a pervasive principle in that it may be applied to all kinds of pollution: vessel-source pollution, atmospheric pollution, pollution caused by dumping, land-based pollution, pollution of inland waters, air pollution, conservation of animal species and flora etc., including wildlife, pollution by toxic or dangerous products and wastes, radioactivity etc.[13] This will remain a major problem for investors and insurers until the possible dimensions of environmental damage and the preventative measures have been explored.

In so far as the European Union is concerned, Article 130r(2) provides, inter alia, that:

> Community policy on the environment shall aim at a high level of protection taking into account the diversity of situations in the various regions of the Community. It shall be based on the precautionary principle and on the principles that preventive action should be taken, that environmental damage should as a priority be rectified at source and that the polluter should pay.

The word 'should' does not make it obligatory for the polluter to pay. Consequently, it is for each Member State of the European Union to decide whether they will implement the 'polluter pays' principle. It is not regarded as a Community obligation. Furthermore, the translated version of Article 130r(2) adopted by the Member States reads differently; for example, whereas Denmark, France, Greece, Italy, the Netherlands, Portugal and Spain provide for the 'polluter pays' principle, Germany has adopted the 'causer' principle. In England, it is not obligatory for the polluter to pay.

The European Union allows national aid for environmental measures, which aid comes out of the Community structural funds. The contradiction in the 'polluter pays' principle in so far as the European Union is concerned is that whereas a Member State may not be paid aid for bringing say, its water quality up to the Community standard, another Member State may receive aid for cleaning the pollution caused by it.

3.3.11 Some Comments on Environmental Risks

Although it is difficult to determine the exact contents and dimensions of the term 'environment' there seems to exist a general awareness of what it entails. Such general awareness or understanding is not sufficiently precise however to determine the liability of a legal person, in law. Nevertheless, two particular dimensions of the issue of the protection, preservation and improvement of the environment seem to have been defined: (a) the provision of a clean environment which would allow human beings to live in dignity and well-being (this idea of maintaining and preserving a clean environment has also been extended to include animal life, sea life and even plant life); and (b) a duty to carry out investment-related work by investors of any kind without causing damage by activities dangerous to the environment.

Human activities and accidents usually give rise to environmental damage. In order to institute a claim, an injury or harm to the claimant must be established. Under customary international law, when an act of a state violates an international obligation, a duty arises to make reparations. The determination of the violation is examined with reference to the principle of state responsibility. Furthermore, at a domestic or regional level, violation of the relevant legislation and duty, may give rise to claims. Most of the claims relating to environmental pollution may encompass negligence, and under common law, actions may therefore be brought in negligence too. The usual elements required for establishing liability are: identification of the wrongdoer, causality, proof, measurement of harm or injury and the degree or nature of fault. Whether the fault was occasioned intentionally or maliciously may be considered, but fault has nothing to do with the intent. It may be considered whether the harm or injury caused by avoidance of or failure to observe an accepted international minimum standard (a duty) is enough to establish liability. Failure to exercise due diligence to avert harm or injury is often applied to establish liability. In the context of commercial or engineering activity, causation of environmental harm or injury by installing, for example, inappropriate technology or by using harmful products or chemicals can satisfy the criterion of 'causality'.

The caution should be entered however that certain international instruments provide for responsibility regardless of preventative measures taken by a state. The Report of the Expert Group on Environmental Protection and Sustainable Development recommended that reparation should be paid to the victims of environmental injury or harm even though the act causing the injury or harm may not be deemed illegal. In other words, in determining environmental liability, the social responsibility of the actor/doer becomes important. Negotiators should therefore be familiar with the practice and policy followed by a host state in respect of absolute liability and strict liability.[14]

The issue of the nexus between the injury or harm and the cause (causality) may sometimes appear to be remote or speculative, but with the advancement of scientific investigation, it may not prove to be so.

Where a pollutant travels a long distance, even crossing territorial boundaries, transnational environmental claims arise; and it seems almost certain that the *Trail Smelter* rule will be applied by courts and tribunals to determine liability, and to assess damages in addition to applying the principles of international responsibility, and the treaty-law, if any bilateral treaty in relation to environmental protection exists between the states concerned.

Environmental pollution can have an adverse effect on vegetation, buildings or other architectural works. Negotiators should take this issue into consideration too. Of course, the problem may remain whether such deterioration was caused by one pollutant emitted by the plant of the actor or in combination with other pollutants for the emission of which the actor should not be held responsible. But, in any event, a degree of causality may be established. Where the author of the pollution is identified and causality established, liability may not be difficult to determine.

The position of transnational corporations in environmental damage cases is well-established. Although they may not have international legal personality, for specific purposes the states of which they are nationals may act on their behalf. This is particularly true of the International Convention on the Settlement of Investment Disputes between States and Nationals of Other States, 1965. Negotiators should find out whether the host state and the state to which the transnational corporation belong are parties to this Convention, and whether a clause will be incorporated whereby disputes arising under that contract will be governed by this Convention. Of course, parties do have the opportunity to be governed by the Convention even after a dispute has actually arisen.

The imputability rule is so well recognised that it is almost certain that a state, the territory of which is usual for the activities causing environmental injury or harm elsewhere or under whose control it occurs, will be held responsible.[15] Conversely, an act of a private foreign investor causing injury or harm to the people of a host country may be imputed to the parent company to establish liability by the imputability theory and by establishing the nature of control exercised by the parent company over its subsidiaries' operation in foreign jurisdictions. Furthermore, by applying the nationality principle of public international law, where a large number of people have suffered injury or harm caused by a foreign entity, the government of that country may take up the action on behalf of its own nationals, and the locus of the injury or harm determines the jurisdiction.[16] The *Amico Cadiz* case[17] was brought by France and the parties injured by the extensive damage caused to the coast of Brittany from the oil tanker spill. In considering the claims submitted by the French government, the cities and towns that were harmed, individuals, fishermen and environmental groups, the US District Court discussed the following categories of damages: loss of enjoyment, loss of reputation, restoration of coastline and harbour, ecological harm, individual claims, costs of cleaning up, cost of material and the equipment purchased for the cleaning up work done.

The issues of absolute liability and strict liability are also relevant to making environmental claims. There are primarily two aspects of environmental damages or injuries: a departure from responsibility or duty, and the consequences of the departure. This is made clear in Article 139 of the UNCLOS (the UN Convention on the Law of the Sea, 1982):

1. States Parties shall have the responsibility to ensure that activities in the Area, whether carried out by States Parties, or State enterprises or natural or juridical persons which possess the nationality of States Parties or are effectively controlled by them or their nationals, shall be carried out in conformity with this part ...

2. Without prejudice to the rules of international law and Annex in Article 22, damage caused by the failure of a State Party or international organisation to carry out its responsibilities under this part shall entail liability; States Parties or international organisations acting together shall bear joint and several liability.[18]

The *Trail Smelter* arbitration[19] between the United States and Canada recognised; that the principle of state responsibility is applicable to issues of trans-boundary pollution in consequence of which states may be held liable to affected private parties and other states sustaining identifiable and sustainable injuries or harm. Furthermore, the duty to refrain from causing further damage also arises. Indemnities were paid by the Trail Smelter Company, a Canadian company, to the US victims of pollution caused by the emission of sulphur dioxide from the plant. But the case was reopened by the US government seeking claim from the Canadian government after the Canadian company installed extra stacks to the plant for increasing their production and thereby caused greater pollution.

Although some of the claims submitted by the US government were not accepted by the tribunal due to lack of evidence, in regard to the others, it decided that in considering such claims account should be taken not only of the existing rules of international law but also the practice existing in the federal states. The tribunal emphasised that there existed a general duty for states to protect other states from harmful or injurious acts by individuals and corporate bodies within their jurisdiction. In rendering its award, the tribunal referred to the topographical, meteorological and economic conditions of the region affected by pollution.

A sufficient number of Conventions, international and regional, have already been concluded to create awareness in societies and private foreign investors; lenders and borrowers are required to pay attention to the norms developed by these instruments. Where the environmental condition is already below acceptable standards, perhaps private foreign investors should in negotiating contracts refer to that in order to ensure that they are not held responsible in cases where further activity will simply aggravate the risk. A warranty to that effect may be regarded as a jeopardising factor in negotiating the deal but precautionary measures in this regard seem to be necessary.

Environmental issues will continue presenting controversy and problems for negotiators for some time to come. Any rigid view on environmental risks will jeopardise the interests of both parties to a prospective contract. Furthermore, parties are required to appreciate that a total avoidance of environmental risks may not be possible in an already polluted environment. Care must be taken to ensure that the risk is not aggravated by the investor.

In arranging project finance, lenders should look into these issues carefully as any litigation concerning the alleged injury caused by the investor prior to its completing the project, may have a bearing upon servicing the loan.

Foolproof environmental risk insurance policies may not be available until all probable aspects of these risks have been identified by scientists. Meanwhile, the 'foreseeability' principle should be applied, bearing in mind that the customary rules of international law are adequate to consider the issues of due diligence, skill and negligence overall, in addition to the existing rules that are operational in a specific jurisdiction.

3.3.12 Expert-dependency Risks

This risk usually becomes evident in countries that lack experts. Even after the completion of a project, experts are needed for its full and effective operation, in consequence of which the project becomes dependent upon foreign experts. Dependence on foreign experts does not present any problem when the political relations between the foreign investor's country and the country of the host contracting party remain friendly, but a deterioration of political relations between these countries may have a damaging effect on the operation of the project.

This is a risk which may be avoided by careful planning. The foreign investor should try to provide experts or even materials (if the latter were a term of the contract) from another jurisdiction in which another subsidiary of the same parent may be operating. Failure to provide experts or materials for the effective operation of a project may be tantamount to derogating from the contractual obligations. This may be explained by means of the case between the *National Oil Corporation (Libya and the Libyan Sun Oil Co. (U.S.)*.[20] Under the Exploration and Production Sharing Agreement of 1980 (EPSA), the Libyan Sun Oil Company (Sun-oil), a Delaware (US) wholly-owned subsidiary of Sun Oil Company Inc., a Pennsylvanian corporation undertook, inter alia, to:

> ... cause its parent and affiliated companies to furnish aid, including technical aid, foreign personnel ... training and services required or requested by Operator or the Management Committee in connection with Petroleum operations.

In 1981, the political relationship between the United States and Libya deteriorated, and in 1982, the US government issued an instruction whereby all US corporations employing US personnel in Libya were required to repatriate them. In compliance with the governmental instruction, Sun-oil and its subcontractors stopped all operational activities in Libya. The Libyan government brought an action against Sun-oil on the ground of the breach of the Agreement, but the US corporation invoked *force majeure*, pointing out that owing to unforeseen circumstances it was not possible for it to perform the Agreement.

The Tribunal found against Sun-oil on the ground that the invocation of *force majeure* was unsustainable as the parent corporation of the foreign subsidiary could have provided experts from its Canadian affiliate in which Sun-oil had 75 per cent of its capital.

The US-Libyan arbitration clearly points to the fact that negotiators of international commercial contracts should avoid the risk of expert dependency by making provision for alternative sources of experts and materials, particularly when a parent operates subsidiaries in other jurisdictions. Of course, this risk may be avoided to a certain extent, and certainly over a period of time by making arrangements for the training of local people.

3.3.13 Calamity Risks

These risks are easily ascertainable by studying whether in the past the host country has been subject to risks, such as natural calamities. Although a natural calamity may suddenly take place without any history of such risks, they are generally foreseeable risks, and negotiators have the choice of deciding whether or not to invest in such countries. If they decide in favour of investing in such countries, they must take adequate protection against such risks, whether by means of insurance policies or otherwise. Invocation of *force majeure* on the ground of calamity risks may not be sustainable. A careful analysis of country profiles should allow a negotiator to learn whether a country is often a victim of calamity risks. On the other hand, where calamity risks are seasonal, sufficient protection against such risks may be taken by an arrangement whereby the progress of work may be suspended during specified period(s) or may be continued with after taking preventative or protective measures, where possible. Additional costs that may be incurred must be taken into account in taking such measures.

3.3.14 War Risks

In the event of an all-out war affecting the host country, the investment process or business may have to be suspended. The host country has however an obligation to draw the attention of the foreign investor to such risks in sufficient time, and where necessary, require the foreign personnel to leave the country until the war is over. Where however a war has been initiated by the host country, the legal position becomes different. The host country will be liable to pay the foreign investor compensation for the injury (damage) she has caused, including the future profit for a designated period.

Hostilities and civil wars are different from wars in the traditional sense of the term. In the case of hostilities and civil wars taking place after a foreign investor or business entity entered into the country, the legal issue which is required to be considered is whether the host country contributed to or whether it failed to exercise due care and diligence in protecting the interests of the foreign investor or business entity and the lives of foreign personnel. This issue entails considerable legal controversy. One of the recent cases on this issue was *Asian Agricultural Products Ltd. and the Republic of Sri Lanka*.[21] In this arbitration, the ICSID tribunal maintained that the causal link between the losses suffered by the foreign investor and the 'combat action' was not conclusive. The question of due diligence was considered by the tribunal with reference to the principal investment treaty existing between the government of the United Kingdom and the Republic of Sri Lanka, and the tribunal pointed out that the onus of proving the failure to exercise 'due diligence' by the host country lay on the claimant, which the latter failed to discharge. The Republic of Sri Lanka was however ordered to pay the foreign investor compensation. It is important for negotiators to consult the principal investment treaties between the two countries, that is, between the government of the investor and that of the host country, and make reference to such treaties in the investment agreement. The caution should be entered that contentions such as 'due diligence' or 'strict liability' are often difficult, although not impossible, to establish by a claimant. Insurance policies covering war risks are available; nevertheless, as with many other risks, parties must ensure that they did not contribute to inflicting injuries on themselves.

Hostilities or civil strife are different from war risks. It must be borne in mind that none of these incidents is comparable to another. Each of these incidents is, so to say, *sui generis* in character. The legal aspects of hostilities or civil strife are different from those of wars, and *force majeure* may not necessarily be invoked to bring a contract to an end.[22]

In the event of any of these risks taking place, the foreign investor, in agreement with the host country or party, should suspend business or investment-related work for a reasonable period of time to see how events progress. This issue should be discussed during the negotiation period. Should, however, the trouble continue for a long time and should it appear that performance of the contract would be absolutely impossible, or its performance at a later date would not produce the desired result, then by mutual consent, the contract may be brought to an end. This issue is also important for submitting a sustainable claim to the insurance company.

3.3.15 *Financial Risk*

Financial risk is caused by a problem in the supply of finance. Usually, the responsibility for the supply of finance is taken by the foreign party or it may be shared by both parties. Often, international agencies, such as the International Bank for Reconstruction and Development or the International Development Agency (IDA) or a regional development bank, such as the Asian Development Bank or the African Development Bank may agree to provide finance for a project. Finance may also be raised by syndicated loans. Incidentally, a private entity may seek finance from the International Finance Corporation (IFC), provided that the project has received support and approval from its government, and that that government belongs to IFC.

Whatever may be the source of finance, parties must ensure that it is available by the stipulated date. In the event of borrowing finance from international agencies, parties are bound by those agencies' rules and regulations. International agencies do not usually provide the agreed amount of finance in one instalment. Finance is usually disbursed by them upon receipt of satisfactory progress reports from the beneficiary.

Syndications also have their own policies as to the grant and disbursements of finance. Where an investor or foreign business entity has undertaken the obligation to provide finance, it must ensure that lack of finance does not hinder or stop the progress of the project, as in that event the host party will have a claim for damages. On the other hand, where a host party has undertaken to provide finance, whether in full or in part, it must do so according to the agreed schedule, otherwise the foreign investor or business entity will exercise its right to claim damages.

Parties should clarify this issue at the negotiation stage, including the penalty or damage clause. Again it is a foreseeable risk, and *force majeure* may not be successfully invoked in such cases to bring the contract to an end.

The technique of negotiating syndicated loan agreements has been discussed in a separate chapter of this work. Availability of finance is often performance-related. Foreign investors and business entities should take special care of this factor. In other words, in order to ensure the availability of finance on a regular basis, the other elements of a contract must also be performed according to schedules. This is why undue dependency on external sources of supply of material or labour or experts should be avoided, where possible.

Where a host country seeks finance from an international or intergovernmental or regional agency, it should familiarise itself first with the criteria it is required to satisfy to be allowed finance by them, and the conditions and formalities that are attached to the grant of finance.[23]

3.4 The Primary Causes of High Incidence of Expropriation of Foreign Assets

A high incidence of expropriation of foreign assets in developing countries became particularly evident during the period 1960–80. The decolonisation process, coupled with the aspiration of the newly-born countries to assert their ownership in natural resources and gradual control over various foreign manufacturing industries, made the incidence of taking foreign assets inevitable. This issue has been discussed in detail in the chapters on negotiation of petroleum agreements and negotiation of mining agreements. International law recognises the right of a sovereign state to take assets in the national interest provided the owner of assets is paid compensation. This is not to suggest that states should be encouraged to expropriate foreign assets, but merely to point out the inevitability of such events. The principle of *pacta sunt servanda* seems to lose its sacrosanct nature when property is taken in the national interest. In the recent past, in the *Aminoil* arbitration,[24] the US corporation relied upon the stabilisation clause in the investment agreement between the parties, but the Government of Kuwait justified its act of taking the assets of and gaining control over the foreign company as a consequence of its economic development programme. In its award, the Tribunal stated, inter alia, that:

> The Tribunal does not see why a Government that was pursuing a coherent policy of nationalisation should not have been entitled to do so progressively. It is hardly necessary, additionally, to stress the reasonable character of a policy of nationalisation operating gradually by successive stages; in step with the developments of the necessary administrative and technical availabilities.[25]

The controversy surrounding the genuineness of the 'public interest' as a ground for taking foreign assets is one which may never be resolved to everybody's satisfaction. In *Luther v. Sagor*, Warrington U said that:

> ... the validity of the acts of an independent sovereign government in relation to property and persons within its jurisdiction cannot be questioned in the Courts of this country.[26]

Of course, the illegality of taking foreign assets, that is, without any public interest ground, is condemned by international law, and customary international law requires the 'taker of property' to pay *lucrum cessans* in addition to *restituto in integrum*.[27]

In the context of this work, there is little point in going into the controversy as to the determination of the amount of compensation in a given case. However, it may be pointed out that this is a risk which all investors should be aware of, and by virtue of its being a foreseeable risk, they should also take precautionary measures. The risk of expropriation of foreign assets should be considered from a practical standpoint.

3.5 Downward Trend in Taking of Foreign Assets

With the conclusion of the major phase of the de-colonisation process, the incidence of taking of foreign assets has significantly diminished. A number of studies have already been carried out on this issue, and mention should be made of those by Hawkins et al.,[28] Jodice,[29] Korbin[30] and Minor.[31] The studies carried out by Korbin and Minor clearly suggest that no expropriation took place in developing countries between 1987 and 1992. Between 1981 and 1986, they suggest, only nine countries expropriated such assets.

It should be noted that many developing countries have accepted the MIGA (Multilateral Investment Guarantee Agency) Convention with a substantial financial stake in the Agency,[32] signifying their commitment to it. The provision of Article 2 of the MIGA Convention is intended:

> ... to encourage the flow of investments for productive purposes among member countries, and in particular to developing member countries, thus supplementing the activities of the International Bank for Reconstruction and Development ... the International Finance Corporation and other international development finance institutions.

Furthermore, the trend of privatisation of state-owned enterprises has already become manifest in the developing world.[33] In fact, this trend seems to have been more common than the trend of nationalisation. Many of the developing countries have been encouraging foreign investors to invest in their jurisdictions with the guarantee that if their assets are expropriated, they will be allowed to buy them back.[34]

The incidence of risks in foreign investments has diminished, although political risk will always remain as a cause of apprehension. However, the reality of this risk must be considered by foreign investors by referring to the pattern of behaviour or the political records, in the context of foreign investment, maintained by a country. On the other hand, intervention in the domestic affairs of one country by another country, or any other action that might jeopardise the friendly relations between any two countries will have a direct adverse effect upon private foreign investment. From this standpoint, it may be maintained that political risk may sometimes be caused by states themselves in consequence of which private foreign investors suffer in foreign jurisdictions. Interaction between governmental authorities and the business community must be close and reality-oriented rather than policy-oriented. To obtain compensation is no substitute for earning profits and contributing to the economy of a country.

3.6 Conclusions

It is possible to classify risks into two broad categories: foreseeable and unforeseeable risks. Most of the risks in business are foreseeable risks. A real risk must be 'unforeseeable'. 'Foreseeability' suggests the capacity of a commercial man to foresee a risk. The risks that are usually included in a *force majeure* clause, for example, are foreseeable risks; therefore they may not be regarded as real risks. 'Unforeseeable risks' present real risks. These risks cannot be foreseen by any prudent commercial man. These risks frustrate contracts.

Where a risk is 'foreseeable' an investor should not invest without protecting his interest, whether by insurance policies or otherwise, and if he does so, then it must be regarded as a self-induced risk. Risks such as those presented by cyclone, storm or other natural causes are not necessarily unforeseeable risks in many cases if an investor carefully studies the country profile, but if such a study did not present any hint of the risk, then of course it is an unforeseeable risk, and the contract will come to an end for reason of impossibility of performance, and not by *force majeure.*

In considering the incidence of risks in investment, negotiators should carry out a feasibility study which should also pay attention to risks; but risks must be studied from a realistic standpoint, rather than from a perspective influenced by historical incidents or unfounded prejudice. It has been explained in this chapter that the incidence of the traditional risks in investment in developing countries over the last decade or so has diminished. Risks should be studied from a practical standpoint.

On the other hand, certain types of investment may present particular risks; for example, to transfer high technology to many of the developing countries may in itself be a risky venture, as many of them lack absorption capacity. Naturally, the return from such capital investment for the investor will be very low if not nil. Risks therefore are to be studied with reference to a particular society and political regime in addition to geographic and climatic conditions. There is no general formula for calculating risks.

Notes

1   U.N. Conference on Environment and Development, 3–14 June,1992, Doc. A'Conf. 151/5/Rev.1 dated 13 June 1992. The text of the Declaration has been reprinted in 31 *International Legal Materials* (1992), 876.
2   See *The Order of the Southern District Court of New York*; reprinted in 25 *International Legal Materials* (1986), 771.
3   See further W. Lang, H. Neuhold and K. Zemanek, *Environmental Protection and International Law*, London, Graham & Trotman (1991).

4   For example the nuclear catastrophe in Chernobyl in 1986 and the catastrophe caused by the pesticide plant, Union Carbide India Limited, in Bhopal, India in 1984.
5   Recommendation C(74)224 adopted on 14 November 1974.
6   EC Commission, 6th *General Report* (1972) at 8.
7   240183 1985 ECR 532.
8   302/86 1988 ECR 4607.
9   For an instructive discussion of the European Environmental Law, see, L. Kramer, *Focus on European Environmental Law*, London, Sweet & Maxwell (1992).
10 Recommendation adopted on 26 May, C(72) 128.
11 Recommendation adopted by the Council on 7 July 1989, C(89)88.
12 Recommendation C(74)224 of 14 November 1974.
13 For a good discussion of the international action taken against environmental damage, see A. Kiss and D. Shelton, *International Environmental Law*, London, Transnational Publishers Inc. (1991).
14 See, in particular, the Convention on International Liability for Damage Caused by Outer Space Object (1972). This Convention was applied to determine the liability caused by the disintegration in the Canadian Space of the Soviet Satellite Cosmos 954 in 1977. See *International Legal Materials* (1981), 689.
15 See however the opinion of the International Law Commission, according to which '... the conduct of a person or a group of persons not acting on behalf of a State shall not be considered as an act of the State ...', Article 11, Report (1980).
16 *In re* Oil Spill by Amoco Cadiz off the Coast of France, March 16, 1978.
17 The Bhopal case.
18 See also Articles 1 and 12 of the Convention on International Liability for Damage Caused by Outer Space Objects, 1972.
19 1931–41, 3 UN RIAA 1905.
20 This case was referred to the Court of Arbitration of the International Chamber of Commerce. The award has been reprinted in 29 *International Legal Materials* (1990), 605.
21 This Award has been reprinted in 30 *International Legal Materials* (1991), 580.
22 This issue has been discussed in a separate chapter.
23 For a detailed discussion of the project cycle (which is usually known as project finance when finance is sought from private institutions) and the formalities that an applicant is required to satisfy for seeking finance from World Bank, see C. Chatterjee, the chapter entitled 'The World Bank' in *International Economic Law and Development in States*, London, The British Institute of International and Comparative Law (1992), pp. 119–45.
24 The Arbitration between the Government of the State of Kuwait and the American Independent Oil Company (AMINOIL), IC5D Arbitration, 24 March 1982, reproduced in 21 *International Legal Materials* (1982), 976.
25 Op. cit., para. 86.
26 *Aksionainove Obschestvo A.M. Luther v. James Sagor & Co.* [1921] 3K.B. 532, 548.
27 For a discussion of the basis for awarding compensation, see the case concerning the *Factory at Chorzo'w* (*Germany v. Poland*) (1928) PCIJ, Series A, No. 17.
28 R.G. Hawkins, N. and M. Provissiero, 'Government Takeovers of US Foreign Affiliates', 7 *Journal of International Business Studies* (1976), 3–16.
29 D. Jodice, 'Sources of Change in Third World Regimes for Foreign Direct Investment, 1968–1976', 34 *International Organization* (1980), 177–206.

30 S.J. Korbin, 'Foreign Enterprises and Forced Divestment in the LDCs', 34 *International Organization* (1980), 65–88; 'Trends in Forced Divestment of Foreign Affiliates, 1960–1979', *The United Nations Centre on Transnational Corporations Reporter* (1982), 13–38; 'Expropriation as an Attempt to Control Foreign Firms in LDCs: Trends from 1960–1979', 3 *International Studies Quarterly* (1984), 329–48; 'Diffusion as an Explanation of Oil Nationalization', 29 *Journal of Conflict Resolution* (1985), 3–12; and 'Testing the Bargaining Hypothesis in the Manufacturing Sector in Developing Countries', 41 *International Organization* (1987), 609–38.
31 M.S. Minor, 'The Demise of Expropriation as an Instrument of LDC Policy, 1980–1992', 25 *Journal of International Business Studies* (1994), 177–88.
32 See S.K. Chatteijee, 'The Convention Establishing the Multilateral Investment Guarantee Agency', 36 *International and Comparative Law Quarterly* (1987), 76–91; see also L. Wallace, 'MIGA: Up and Running', *Finance and Development* (1992), 4849.
33 See R. Condoy-Sekse, Techniques of Privatisation of State-owned Enterprises: Inventory of Country Experience (vol. 11), Washington, DC, World Bank (1988); W. Glade, *Privatisation of Public Enterprises in Latin America*, San Francisco, International Center for Economic Growth (1991); R. Kikeri, J. Nellis and M. Shirley, *Privatisation: The Lessons of Experience*, Washington, DC, The World Bank (1992); M. Minor, *Privatisation: A Worldwide Summary*, Report Prepared for the Transnational Corporations and Management Division of the United Nations, New York (1993); R. Ramamurti, 'Why are Developing Countries Privatising?', 23 *Journal of International Business Studies* (1992), 225–49; R. Ramamurti and R. Vernon (eds), *Privatisation and Control of State-owned Enterprises*, Washington, DC, The World Bank (1991); and C. Vuylsteke, *Techniques of Privatisation of State-owned Enterprises* (vol. 1): *Methods and Implementation*, Washington, DC, The World Bank (1988).
34 T. Kamm, 'Argentina Offers YPF SA to Local Foreign Investors', *Wall Street Journal*, June (1993), A12; see also R. Holman, 'Zambia's Privatisation Program', *Wall Street Journal*, March (1993), A6; J. Tanner, 'Venezuela Starts to Bring Back Foreign Oil Firms', *Wall Street Journal*, March (1993), A8; D. Solis, 'As Mexico's Pemex nears Privatisation, Foreign Energy Firms Gear up to Drill', *Wall Street Journal*, August (1992), AS.

4 Negotiation of International Sales Contracts

4.1 Introduction

Sales contracts in this context stand for contracts for the sale of any product or commodity. Depending upon the nature of the commodity or product, some special terms and conditions are required to be included in contracts. However, certain common terms and conditions are generally relevant to all sales contracts. Again, the special terms and conditions of sales, where relevant, should be considered by a team prior to its leaving for a foreign country contract.

This chapter is based on the assumption that goods will be bought and sold on a c.i.f (cost, insurance and freight) basis and the two parties are located in two different jurisdictions. A c.i.f. contract is, in reality, a combination of three contracts: (a) the goods contract; (b) the payment contract; and (c) the carriage of goods (transportation) contract. The most important issues in relation to each of these subcontracts are discussed in this chapter. In all contracts of sale, the following are the prime issues which should be negotiated upon: the goods, the time of delivery, the place of delivery, the methods of payment, replacement and service of equipment and settlement of disputes. Each of these items is now briefly discussed to provide the reader with some basic information on these terms. For further information, the reader should consult standard books on export trade.[1]

4.2 The Goods

Goods means the goods which are intended to be bought and sold. No negotiation process should be embarked upon until the parties are certain of the goods to be bought and sold. In other words, the prospective buyer must specify his requirements, and the prospective seller must ensure that he can supply the goods specified by the prospective buyer. Similar goods will not do. If a prospective seller wishes to provide similar goods then he should notify the prospective buyer accordingly. Parties should not try to negotiate on what may be supplied and received; instead they should settle this issue before coming to the negotiating table.

The buyer should state the purpose for which the goods may be used so that the prospective seller may obtain or order or manufacture the goods accordingly. It is the prospective buyer's duty to provide the prospective seller with the precise specifications of the goods, unless the prospective buyer has openly agreed that the choice of goods may be made by the prospective seller.

In the case of goods/machinery sought by tender, the specifications are provided by the prospective buyer at the time of sending application forms to the prospective offerees. Specifications must include all details of the goods, e.g. volume, weight voltage where relevant, quality and the purpose for which the goods/machinery may be used.

Description of goods should also clearly indicate the quality and standard, the latter specified by a particular institution, that the buyer requires. If goods are meant for a variety of uses, the prospective buyer must draw the prospective seller's attention to that effect.

As for the prospective seller, he must ensure that he will be in a position to supply the goods specified by the prospective buyer and that the goods may be used for the purposes for which the prospective buyer wishes to buy them. In fact, where a prospective buyer has failed to mention the probable use of the goods, a prudent prospective seller should nevertheless ask the prospective buyer about the uses for which the latter wishes to buy the goods.

If goods have several components or parts, each part must conform to the specification given by the prospective buyer. If the buyer has asked for a special packaging for the goods, the seller must provide that; otherwise, the packaging generally used in the commercial world for that kind of goods will do. If goods are to be delivered in a particular form or package, such as 12 in a container they must be delivered precisely in that form.

As stated earlier, depending upon the nature of the goods, the prospective buyer and the prospective seller should achieve clarification of certain essential issues pertaining to the goods prior to their meeting at the negotiating table. The prospective seller should also ensure that he does not invite a case of 'product liability' on himself.

4.3 Time of Delivery

This is an issue which is usually settled at the negotiating table. However, before leaving for negotiation, the prospective seller should have an idea about the time-scale required for delivery of the goods. If the goods are to be manufactured in another country, sufficient time allowance should be made. In fact, the buyer should be notified of that fact as any delay caused by the manufacturer will be attributed to the seller. It is possible to notify the buyer of the source of the goods, without disclosing the actual manufacturer. Of course, a provision to this effect should be made in the contract.

Sometimes the time for delivery is so crucial that it is regarded as an important term of the contract. If the prospective buyer insists on the prospective seller's delivery of the goods on a particular date, for whatever reason, and the seller accepts that, failure to perform the contract on that day will amount to a breach of the contract. At the negotiation point therefore, the parties should seek either a specific date or a time frame with a proviso that a specific date for delivery will be determined within a reasonable period of time. Parties should ensure that the actual date of delivery does not fall on a local holiday.

4.4 Place of Delivery

Buyers usually want their goods delivered at their place of business; alternatively, they may choose another place for delivery of the goods. This is a matter over which the prospective buyer has for obvious reasons more command than the prospective seller, although the latter has the right to raise objection to delivering the goods at a particular location whether for logistical reasons or otherwise, and in the latter event, the location of delivery must be mutually agreed upon.

4.5 The Payment Contract

4.5.1 Method(s) of Payment

When export sales contracts are concluded on c.i.f. terms, payment is usually made through the documentary credit mechanism, that is, through letters of credit. This is not the appropriate place to describe the documentary credit mechanism;[2] however a few important issues that often give rise to legal problems may be identified and briefly discussed. First, the currency in which payment should be made by the buyer: the seller may favour payment in a particular hard currency, but depending upon the exchange rate between that chosen currency and the buyer's currency, the seller may have to settle for another hard currency. The seller may favour payment in his own hard currency as it will preclude his paying for conversion. Of course, choice of currency of payment does not present any problem when trade is operated between two rich countries, as exchange regulations in such countries either are not operational or even if operational, restrictions on remittance of funds are minimal. By virtue of the operation of the principle of free movement of capital, trade among the European Union States is not subject to any exchange control regulations.

Second, the prospective buyer and seller should carefully choose the location of the advising/confirming bank as in the event of a legal dispute arising under the letter of credit contract, it is the location of negotiation and payment that determines the governing law of the contract. Therefore, if parties are not familiar with the governing law of the location, they should not elect the advising/confirming bank in that location.

The third issue concerns which the seller may be required to submit to the issuing bank in compliance with the buyer's instruction, as a condition of payment. The seller must comply with that instruction and the documents, particularly the bill of lading (the document that passes the title in goods to a buyer) must be clean and without any encumbrances. Where, for example, the buyer has asked for two expert certificates, in confirmation of the quality of the goods, the seller must comply with the condition. Documents must be exact documents, and not similar documents.

Fourth, the maturity time of the credit – the export sales contract should clearly specify that it is a c.i.f contract and that in so far as payment through the letter of credit mechanism is concerned the parties will be governed by the Uniform Commercial Practice (UCP) published by the International Chamber of Commerce. It is to be pointed out that both parties must ensure that their governments have accepted the UCP (latest revision).

4.5.2 Other Methods of Payment

Various other methods of payment are also available in export trade, namely, open account, advance payment, letter of credit, and countertrade (including buy-back, switch trading and evidence account). These are now briefly discussed.

4.5.2.1 Open account Under this arrangement, the seller is required to send goods and the document of title (bill of lading) for each shipment direct to the buyer. The buyer undertakes to settle the account at a predetermined future date. The open account system is operated on a trust basis; that is, the undertakings of each party are accepted on trust, and each party is required to fulfil its obligation. This system allows the seller to produce/manufacture goods in advance for a secure buyer, and the buyer will have sufficient time to find prospective buyers too. This system of payment can operate very well between countries that are not subject to foreign exchange regulations. Details of accounts are sent to buyers by sellers on a regular basis so that the buyer is aware of the payment position, and payments are often made by bank transfers. This method of payment is usually adopted by business houses that have been known to each other for a considerable period of time or have trust in each other's integrity. Some risks are nevertheless involved in this method of payment: the buyer may fail to honour its obligation, and the seller may lose control over its goods and title in them; otherwise between known parties the system seems to work well.

4.5.2.2 Advance payment Payment in advance is preferred by any exporter, although, in reality, very few buyers would be prepared to accept this method of payment, as funds will be locked away for future business, which could otherwise have been utilised for more urgent transactions However, under this system, it is possible to make payments in part. Again, this method of payment is possible when the seller's and the buyer's countries do not maintain foreign exchange regulations. In adopting this method of payment, a buyer should ensure that the seller will not be subject to any export prohibitions. Under this method, payment can be made by cheque or by banker's draft or by mail or cable transfer or by international money order, although usually, payment by bank transfer is the preferred method of payment. Under this method of payment, the buyer however runs the risk of breach by the exporter, and therefore, buyers should ask for security against nondelivery of goods, or take out insurance policies against such risks.

4.5.2.3 Payment under a Letter of Credit This is one of the most popular methods of payment in export trade. Under this system, the buyer instructs its banker to remit money to the seller's bank only after the said bank has produced to the issuing bank (the buyer's bank) the documents stipulated by the buyer. The usual documents are: an invoice, a bill of lading and an expert certificate. Experts' certificates are usually sought in order to ensure that the goods are of standard or contract quality. Of course, a buyer can ask for any other document that he may require for the purpose of importation of the goods. Banks operate as the safety institutions for both parties. Export under the letter of credit system is primarily operated on the basis of documents rather than of goods, that is, the documents must represent the goods, so that the sub-buyer may buy them on the basis of the genuineness of the documents representing the goods. Payment under a c.i.f (cost, insurance and freight) contract is usually made by this method, which is also known as the documentary credit method of payment. Documentary credits may be of two types: revocable and irrevocable. A *revocable* credit does not give any undertaking to the seller that payment will actually be made; therefore, it is highly unlikely that a prudent seller will accept this type of credit. An *irrevocable* credit, on the other hand, may not be revoked, and sellers feel assured of payment and can start producing/manufacturing goods on the basis of the credit. A revocable credit may be amended or cancelled only with the consent of all parties concerned.

An irrevocable credit may be confirmed or unconfirmed. Obviously, all exporters will prefer an irrevocable and a confirmed credit. In negotiating credits, the parties to a contract should consider the following:

(a) the amount of the credit and the currency in which it is to be paid;
(b) the type of credit (revocable or irrevocable, confirmed or unconfirmed);
(c) details of documents to be presented by the exporter;
(d) the name of the person on whom the draft is to be drawn and the nature of the draft (sight or tenor);
(e) details of goods;
(f) nature of shipment (transhipment or part-shipment);
(g) the ports of shipment and discharge;
(h) last date of shipment; and
(i) the expiry date of the credit.

The documentary credit system cannot operate between parties unless the governments to which they belong have accepted the Uniform Commercial Papers (UCP) issued by the International Chamber of Commerce. The current UCP 500 (revised) was issued in 1993. In the event of their being governed by it the parties should mention this in their contract.

4.5.2.4 Countertrade This system is adopted to avoid payment in currency. It is very helpful for those countries that have foreign exchange regulations and that suffer from high import costs. Under this arrangement, an exporter can sell its products provided it agrees to import certain products from the same market. Many countries have now adopted regulations as regards countertrade; consequently, exporters will be governed by those regulations if they wish to trade on a countertrade basis. This system is goods-based. Countertrade is extremely helpful for protecting or stimulating domestic industries; and for engaging in international trade which would otherwise not be possible owing to lack of finance.

One should not think that countertrade is exclusive to developing countries; Australia and New Zealand have a mandatory countertrade requirement to offset public sector purchases. It has become a common method of settling accounts in the oil producing countries in exchange for manufactured goods. Countertrade is extremely popular in the COMECON countries; in fact, it constitutes about 25 per cent of their trade with the developed countries.

Brazil, India, Mexico, South Korea and Taiwan find countertrade a very useful means of gaining access to the markets in the West. On the other hand, in countries such as Canada, Chile, Hungary, Kenya, Norway, Paraguay, Switzerland and Zimbabwe countertrade is not officially encouraged, although it is not totally opposed. In reality, countertrade runs counter to the multilateral trading system advocated by GATT/WTO; however, in practice, this method of trading has now been accepted as a legitimate one.

4.6 A Brief Discussion of the Most Popular Types of Countertrade

4.6.1 Counterpurchase

Under this mechanism, an exporter is required to purchase (counterpurchase) goods or services from the buyer's country on condition that the buyer's country gives that seller an export contract. The goods purchased and sold are usually unrelated goods. Under this arrangement, two parallel but separate contracts are concluded, one of which relates to the principal order which is settled in cash or on credit terms, and the other is performed on counterpurchase terms. The value of the counterpurchase, which may not equate with the value of the principal order, is negotiated by the parties concerned. Save the payment system, the contract of counterpurchase otherwise includes most of the usual terms of an export trade contract, namely, time and date of delivery, description of goods, breach, non-performance etc.

Under this arrangement, a developing country usually imports first and exports later. The price of imports is usually met by the gains from exports. With the imports a developing country should be able to manufacture products which will have a market in the foreign jurisdiction; thus there will be no adverse effect on the balance of payments of the country. Counterpurchase obligations may be assigned to third parties, who are paid by the countertrade partner an amount equal to the discount in addition to other agreed expenses.

It is important for parties to find out the countries that support a mandatory counterpurchase system. The countries that operate a counterpurchase system mandatorily, such as Indonesia, have already adopted standard contracts of counterpurchase. There are of course certain countries, such as India and Malaysia, that do not follow a mandatory counterpurchase system. Under the mandatory system, a countertrade clause is often included in tender documents for major governmental procurements from foreign suppliers.

4.6.2   Barter

Under this arrangement, goods and services are exchanged for goods and services. In respect of barter-based transactions, no cash payment is involved. Countertrade in the form of barter is operated between governments. Unlike counterpurchase, in the case of barter, a developing country usually exports first, although an opposite situation is also possible. In view of the inherent flexibility in barter trade, governments seems to prefer it. It must be maintained however that when trade is conducted on the basis of exchange of goods or services, mathematical precision may not be expected; parties seem to be prepared to accept a degree of approximation or margin on either side. It is possible to operate this form of countertrade so that one party is allowed to import first on condition of future export of goods.

4.6.3   Buyback

Supply of capital plant and/or equipment is the usual subject matter of the buyback arrangement. As the term suggests, under this arrangement, the exporter of capital plant or equipment buys back a predetermined quantity of the product from the buyer to offset against the latter's debt. It has become a practice in the developing world to adopt this system of countertrade. This arrangement makes a guaranteed export market available for the exporter (which is usually a developing country). The buyback system becomes an integral part of turn key contracts. The exporter of capital plant or equipment is required to be very understanding in that it may not be able to buyback any product until the factory or the plant has commenced manufacturing products. Under this arrangement, the supplier of capital plant or equipment also gains by availing itself of the opportunity of buying products useful for its home market at a cheaper price. In order to protect against the risks occasioned by a long time lag between the supply of equipment and the actual commencement of production (whether changes are occasioned by political factors or otherwise), exporters of capital plant or equipment should take out insurance policies. A long time lag may also require the parties to renegotiate certain terms of the contract. The risks that are usually associated with turn-key arrangements are the following:

(a) fluctuations in exchange rates or value of the price of buyback products may affect the business, unless a clause protecting the parties against such risks has been incorporated in the contract;
(b) delays in the construction or operation of the plant may require renegotiation of the terms of the contract;
(c) because of the long time lag, products may require improvement or modification to achieve marketability.

However, despite these disadvantages aid agencies, such as the World Bank Group, encourage governments to conclude such contracts when they take loans from them, as they do not adversely affect the balance of payments of countries.

4.6.4 Evidence Accounts

The purpose is to evidence accounts in relation to transactions based on counterpurchase effected by a transnational corporation in a developing country. An arrangement may be established whereby a transnational corporation's subsidiary operating in a developing country will be required to counterpurchase the host country's products equivalent to the imports it has made for its own business. The money thus spent will be debited to the imports, and the amounts earned will be credited to exports; then the difference, if any, will be settled by the party concerned. In practice, it is difficult to identify the price item by item. Peru often engages in countertrade on this basis, particularly with the US transnational corporations.

Negotiation of International Sales Contracts 55

4.6.5 Switch Trading

This form of trading stands for switching or swapping trade. In the event of a credit surplus occasioned by trade between two countries, under this arrangement a third country may take advantage of the surplus. The arrangement may be explained in the following way: Country A's exports to country B created a credit surplus in favour of A. Country C's exports to country A might be financed from the sale of B's goods to country C. A triangular negotiation is essential in effecting such an arrangement. This arrangement entails a number of buyers and sellers, and obviously sales under it involve transfer of documents relating to the goods. Such arrangements are usually made by brokers, who render services for commission.

4.6.6 Offset

The system of offset is often used in relation to deals in high technology, defence materials and equipment. One of the conditions under this arrangement is that the importing country is allowed to offset debt by requiring the exporter to procure components from within the importing country. This has many advantages, namely, the balance of payments position will not be strained; the indigenous people will be compelled to develop components; and they will eventually attain expertise and technological self-sufficiency. There are various forms of offset, but two of the most common are: (a) direct offset and (b) indirect offset.

When an exporter is required to manufacture components for the industry in the importing country and provide technical assistance, then it may be explained as a case of direct offset. Indirect offset occurs where the exporter agrees to accept unrelated products from the importing country. An indirect offset may be described as another version of counterpurchase. This arrangement helps a developing country to develop markets for those products in which she possesses expertise. Offset is also used by developed countries.

4.7 Some Important Points to be Considered in Relation to Countertrade

(a) justification for adopting this method of business;
(b) form of countertrade;

(c) countertrade must be operated in accordance with the policy of the country (whether as an exporter or as an importer);
(d) role of the public sector;
(e) role of the private sector;
(f) types of trading partners (government, semi-government body or a private body);
(g) products involved in countertrade for both import and export – products are specified by the country concerned;
(h) track record of the country in countertrade;
(i) intermediaries who may be involved in countertrade and their track records; and
(j) the terms and conditions of the countertrade contract, including the terms relating to the method(s) of settling disputes.

4.8 Carriage of Goods (Transportation) Contract

In c.i.f. sales, it is for the seller to arrange transportation of goods. The port of destination of goods must be mutually settled between the two parties. In choosing a port, attention should be paid to whether the carrier may experience any difficulty in reaching it. However, the terms and conditions of this contract are not decided by the seller and the buyer. The seller usually contacts a shipping agent for the transportation of goods and transnational carriage of goods is governed by standard charterparties.

4.9 Replacement and Service

Where sales relate to equipment or machinery, it is important to negotiate the terms of service and replacement and incorporate them in the contract. Of course, in most cases, warranties are attached to equipment or machinery. Nevertheless, an offer of servicing the equipment or machinery is not only helpful but also has become common practice. Sometimes a buyer may wish to build a team of trained people of his own, who may be able to service the equipment or machinery in due course. Thus a training programme may also be negotiated and may be attached to the main contract. This issue has been discussed in detail in the chapter dealing with turn-key contracts.

4.10 Negotiation for the Sale of Second-hand/Used Products

Negotiations with a view to selling second-hand goods or equipment are more difficult than negotiations with a view to selling new products and/or equipment in that the seller must be prepared to disclose the state of the goods or equipment in all aspects, and the buyer may insist on a disclosure declaration. Whereas a disclosure declaration may not present much problem, the seller should be careful in giving guarantee as to the state of equipment or goods unless he has evidence to reply upon in support of his guarantee. This is where a tactful negotiation technique is necessary so as to ensure that the prospective buyer is not misled by a misrepresentation of the quality or performance level of the equipment or machinery. Under English law, 'satisfactory quality' is enough, but that may not be so, when equipment or machinery is sold to a foreign buyer. The negotiating team should consist of expert engineers who can honestly and openly explain the quality and performance level of the equipment or machinery.

Negotiation of other terms and conditions, namely method(s) of payment, place of delivery, or time of delivery etc. is similar to that followed in respect of purchase of new products, machinery or equipment which has already been discussed in this chapter.

4.11 Conclusions

The list of items to negotiate on cannot be exhausted. Depending upon the nature of the product or equipment, the negotiating team should list the items which they should discuss with the other party. When all possible terms have been discussed, they should then draft the terms with the help of a lawyer. The role that a lawyer should play in the negotiation of commercial contracts has been discussed in the Conclusions section of this work.

Notes

1 *Schmitthof's Export Trade: The Law and Practice of International Trade*, J. Adams, London, Stevens & Sons (1990).
2 For a good discussion of the documentary credit mechanism, see *UCP 500*, published by the International Chamber of Commerce, Paris (1994).

5 Negotiation of Transfer of Technology Contracts

5.1 Introduction

The term 'technology' is derived from the Greek word 'tekhnelogos' which comprises of two elements: *tekhne* – are and *logos* – treatise. In other words, it stands for the body of knowledge pertaining to equipment or machinery. The term 'tekhne' also embraces the concept of communication of professional knowledge and skills, which are transferable. Transfer of technology therefore means transfer of knowledge and skills. Depending upon the complexity of the equipment, the issue of transfer of knowledge and skills may become difficult to resolve. In many cases, monopolistic regimes may be maintained by the inventors of machinery or equipment. Technology may be transferred in two contexts:

(a) when knowledge and skills relate to known equipment or machinery and are not protected by any monopolistic regime: in such cases, the channels are:

  (I) the movement of experts from one country to another;
  (II) vocational training and instruction;
  (III) exchange of information and of persons under technical cooperation programmes; and
  (IV) dissemination of published materials.

(b) Where technology (equipment or machinery) is owned by a company or corporation, it is protected by industrial patent rights, and its transfer is effected at a price, which is a matter of negotiation. However, in such a situation, transfer entails the following:

  (I) the functions of the machinery/equipment with related documents;

(II) the grant of licences, including manufacturing processes, the use of trade marks, patents etc.;
(III) the use of experts, including their advice; and
(IV) foreign direct investment.

Technology may be bought and sold in any of the following forms:

(a) capital goods (otherwise known as incorporated technology) or intermediate goods associated with an investment;
(b) technical or commercial data freely available on the market (otherwise known as non-incorporated technology) or an exclusive property of an enterprise, the sale of which is subject to restrictions; and
(c) labour, both skilled and specialist, capable of putting the materials and techniques to their most profitable use, and of generating information and resolution of problems.

5.2 The Important Elements of a Contract for the Transfer of Technology

On what basis technology may be transferred is a matter that must be determined by the transferor and the transferee. This is normally done by identifying each other's needs and terms. These issues and terms are discussed at the negotiation stage. Furthermore, local legislation relating to import of technology, including the use of foreign trade marks, patents, designs etc. in addition to that governing the transfer of foreign exchange and employment of foreign labour must be looked into.

The following are regarded as the principal elements of a contract for transfer of technology:

(a) details of engineering works for the installation of facilities for manufacture of products;
(b) licence for the use or exploitation of patents, drawings and industrial models;
(c) licence for the use or exploitation of trade marks and emblems;
(d) agreement to provide technical knowledge through plans, diagrams, models, formulae, training of personnel;
(e) agreement to provide technical assistance on agreed matters; and

(f) agreement to provide service relating to the operation and administration of the programme.

The principal elements of such contracts therefore relate to two aspects: (i) industrial property (points (b) and (c)); and (ii) other aspects specific to technology (points (a), (d), (e) and (f)). The question of acquiring ownership in industrial property rights would not normally arise; such rights are transferred, whereas transference of knowledge amounts to sale of knowledge. Knowledge is transferred by means of technical assistance, diagrams, plans etc.; such knowledge is not protected by any patent or distinguished by any trade mark. A transfer of technology contract therefore, in effect, contains two contracts: (a) contract of use; and (b) contract of ownership.

5.3 Contents of the Contract

Depending upon the nature of technology to be transferred, the terms and conditions of the contract are determined. Nevertheless, it is possible to identify the clauses that are usually included in such contracts:

5.3.1 The Preamble

In addition to including the names of the parties and the date of concluding the contract, the Preamble to such contracts affirms the fact that the licensor has developed certain methods, techniques or formulae in manufacturing certain products and possesses substantial valuable knowledge relating to operational and technical aspects of such methods, techniques or formulae. The trade mark which the licensor uses for its product must also be clearly identified. The Preamble also affirms the desire of the licensee to obtain, and the willingness of the licensor to grant a licence for specified industrial property rights, to supply certain know-how, technical information and to render technical assistance to enable the licensee to manufacture the product. A statement is often included to the effect that it will be of mutual advantage for the licensor to grant the licensee an exclusive or nonexclusive right to manufacture and sell the product. It is crucially important to mention in the Preamble that the licensor has developed a particular formula etc. and that it possesses specialised knowledge in it, and that it has agreed to transfer that knowledge and to manufacture and sell the product(s).

5.3.2 Definitions

This clause should include definitions of all technical and nontechnical terms which may have to be referred to when interpretation of the contractual obligations is necessary. The following are the items, definitions of which are usually included in this clause:

> technology, patent, trade marks, know-how, improvement (any technological advance which is not reflected in an invention or industrial design which is the subject of the patent, but which is presentable), licensed product, licensed territory, licensed sales territory, contract products, technical documentation, contract factory, net selling price, technical service, commercial production, technical information, industrial property rights and the date on which the contract will come into force (the date of effectiveness).

5.3.3 Scope of the Contract

This clause delimits the ambit of the contract by providing that the licensor has agreed to transfer to licensee, and that the licensee has agreed to obtain from the licensor the technical know-how to design, manufacture, install and sell the contract products. Name, model, specifications etc. should be detailed in an Annex.

It is stated that the licensor has agreed to grant the licensee the licence and the right to design, use, manufacture, sell and export on an exclusive or nonexclusive basis within a specified geographic area.

The responsibility of the licensor to send his technical personnel to the licensee for explaining technical documentation and to provide technical instruction and service on design, manufacturing, inspection and test of the contract products must be clearly stated.

A provision must be made for arranging technical training of the licensee's personnel in the latter's factory or at other agreed premises so as to ensure that the licensee's personnel have attained sufficient expertise to operate the programme effectively. Details of training are included in an Annex.

The obligation of the licensor to supply the licensee with the parts and raw materials at the most favourable price whenever the licensee may so require is to be stated. The licensee's right to use the licensor's trade mark on the products must be stated, but it must be so used under the licence of the licensor. In many cases, the buy-back provision for the licensor is also entered in this clause, and where such a provision is included, a separate clause for 'buy-back' should be incorporated in the contract. The provisions for technical information and technical assistance should be as clear as possible.

Sometimes the above items are detailed as obligations of the licensor, under separate headings.

5.3.4 Price of or Consideration for the Contract

This clause may be very detailed or not so detailed. The practice of the Government of the People's Republic of China has been to include a detailed clause on this issue. Many contracts however contain a rather brief clause. In order to avoid future problems, it is better to make this clause as detailed as possible. The usual items that should be included in this clause are the following: the total contract price and the currency in which it will be paid; technology transfer fee, design fee, technical documentation fee, personnel training fee, royalty and the rate of commencement of payment of royalty, the basis for calculating royalty (whether in terms of net selling price of the contract products sold over a year or whether the contract products not sold shall be included). The specific methods adopted for calculating the net selling amount and royalty are usually detailed in an Annex to the contract. The date by which the royalty must be paid is stated in this clause. The fee for the technical service and personnel training is also included in it.

The licensor's right to demand audited accounts of the licensee is usually reserved, and the period of notice for this purpose specified. The initial payment of the contract is fixed, as is the date of settling accounts each year.

5.3.5 Conditions of Payment

The licensor must state the method of payment, whether by mail transfer through a named bank, or otherwise, in addition to providing for the expenses to be borne by the licensee in its own country, and those outside the country. The amount to be paid to the licensor in percentage terms of the total contract price by a stipulated date is included in this clause and the receipt of stipulated documents upon which payment will be made. These documents normally include a valid export license or a photocopy of it issued by the appropriate authorities of the licensor (or that no export licence is required); one original of the irrevocable letter of guarantee issued by the licensor's bank for a stipulated sum in favour of the licensee (a specimen of the letter of guarantee is detailed in an Annex); proforma invoices covering the total contract price; the sum of money in the stipulated currency in percentage terms after the licensor has delivered the final batch of the technical documentation.

This clause also stipulates that the licensee will make payments only after the contract products have been found up to the standard stipulated. Payment of the royalty is conditional upon receipt of the following documents from the licensor: statement of calculation of royalty and an invoice. The licensee reserves its right to deduct from any payment due to the licensor if the licensor should fail to perform its obligation in any way.

5.3.6 Tests and Acceptances

It is the licensor's duty to send representative(s) to test and inspect the contract products in conjunction with the technical personnel of the licensee in the contract factory. This serves the purpose of verifying the accuracy and reliability of the technical documentation supplied by the licensor. After the accuracy and reliability of the technical documentation have been established, the representatives of both parties must sign copies of the acceptance certificate for the contract products and retain these for future reference, if necessary. Provision should be made as to what action should be taken in the event of the contract products failing to achieve the appropriate technical performance.

Where contract products fail to achieve appropriate technical performance after a subsequent attempt, the licensor must compensate the licensee for the losses suffered by the latter. In fact, in such an event, the licensee will have the right to terminate the contract, and claim compensation. On the other hand, if the contract products' failure to achieve the desired technical performance is contributed to by the licensee, then the licensor may have a claim against the licensee or they may be engaged in further negotiation with a view to reaching a resolution.

5.3.7 Delivery of Technical Documents

The location and date of delivery by the licensor to the licensee must be fixed. It should be clearly stated that the risk of technical documents shall be transferred from the licensor to the licensee once the documents have been transferred to the latter. Receipt of these documents must be confirmed whether upon signature on the airway bill or on other documents of transportation. If such documents have not been delivered in perfect condition, the licensee will have the right to seek replacement by a certain date. Usually, the manner of packaging and the identification of packaging by number, weight, consignee code etc. are also stipulated in this clause.

5.3.8 Technical Assistance and Training of Personnel

This clause details the nature of technical assistance required by the licensee. Details of training of the local personnel should also be negotiated and included in this clause. Usually, such details are detailed in the form of an Annex. Provision is often made for training of local people both in the localities of the licensor and of the licensee. The details of remuneration of the experts who may be appointed for training should also be included in this clause.

The licensee must also undertake to facilitate visas (both entry and re-entry), arrange accommodation etc. for the foreign experts, as the licensor will also undertake similar obligations. As to the terms and conditions of work of foreign experts, the reader's attention is drawn to the chapter entitled Negotiation of Service Contracts.

5.3.9 Use of Trademark and Brand Name

In this clause the licensor is required to grant either an exclusive or a nonexclusive, nonassignable licence to use the licensed trademarks during the subsistence of the agreement. The licensor must also be asked not to grant any other party the use of the licensed trademark in the contract territory.

5.3.10 Patent Infringement

Under this clause, the licensee attempts to protect its position against possible infringements of patents. During negotiation therefore the licensor must confirm that it has the right to transfer the ownership of all the technical know-how and documentation to the licensee, and that in the event of a third party bringing any charge of infringement, the licensor shall be responsible for dealing with that issue and that the licensee shall have no responsibility for the claim from that third party.

5.3.11 Confidentiality

The licensee is required to agree that without the prior written consent of the licensor, he shall not sell, assign or divulge the technical information to anybody in any manner except to its employees and subcontractors who will be required to use such information for the purpose of manufacturing the licensed products. It is often stated that the licensee shall have the right to use the know-how and technical documentation provided by the licensor and design, and manufacture and sell the contract products after the termination of the contract.

5.3.12 Taxes and Duties

The licensor ensures that the taxes and duties in connection with and in the implementation of the contract that may be levied by the host state shall be paid by the licensee. On the other hand, all duties and taxes that may be levied by the home state of the licensor for the purpose of entering into the agreement shall be paid by the licensor.

5.3.13 Sub-licensing and Transfer

It is made clear whether the licensee shall or shall not be authorised to sub-license the technical know-how to third parties or whether the contract may be transferred unilaterally by the licensee without the prior consent of the licensor. It is a rather tricky issue in that sub-licensing or transfer may give rise to other problems, particularly in respect of the use of patents and trademarks.

5.3.14 Supply of Components and Materials

Provision is made for the supply of component, parts and raw materials by the licensor to the licensee upon the latter's written request at an agreed price.

5.3.15 Improvements

The purpose of this clause is to clarify that in the event of a party's discovering or coming into possession of any improvements relating to the licensed products or in connection with the design, manufacture, use or sale of the same, at any time during the term of the agreement, that party shall furnish the other party with information on such improvements without any delay or charge.

5.3.16 Guarantees as to the Quality of Technical Documents

This clause secures guarantees as to the quality of technical documentation to be supplied by the licensor to the licensee. The licensee takes guarantees from the licensor to the effect that the licensor must supply the licensee the latest technical documentation initially and as and when it is improved and developed during the terms of the agreement. Furthermore, the licensor is required to give an undertaking that the technical documentation it will supply to the licensee will be complete, correct and that it will be delivered by the stipulated date(s), and that in the event of their not being in conformity with the stipulations, the licensor shall provide conformed documentation, free of charge, by another stipulated date. Many licensees make elaborate provisions in regard to this issue, whereby the detailed obligations of the licensor, and the legal effect of its failure to supply are stated, including the provision for financial penalty for any late delivery of such documentation.

The period for which the performance guarantee supplied by the licensor to the contract factory remains valid must also be clearly stated. The parties also make provision for the termination of the contract, if the licensor should fail to provide stipulated technical documentation by a certain agreed date and the damages that the licensor may be liable to pay the licensee. Similarly, provisions for remedial measures are made if some parts of the contract products are not found to be of contract standard.

This clause often includes the buy-back provisions, whereby the licensor undertakes to buy from the licensee a stipulated amount of the contract products every year. Details of this arrangement are usually incorporated in an Annex.

5.3.17 Export Right

Under this clause the licensee secures its right to export the products to countries in which exclusive licence to use the technology has already been granted, but not to those countries in which such exports will result in an infringement of either party's industrial property rights.

5.3.18 Force Majeure

It has been a common practice to include a *force majeure* clause in almost all commercial contracts, including contracts of transfer of technology. Perhaps a clause entitled 'breach of contract' instead would serve the purpose better in that once impossibility of performance of the contractual obligations by either of the parties has been established, the contract will automatically come to an end. Where however parties have decided to include a *force majeure* clause, the circumstances in which this clause will be activated are usually identified. The usual circumstances are: war, severe flood, typhoon, earthquake or any other circumstance that the parties may have agreed upon. This clause must also identify the duties of each party in the event of invoking *force majeure*. Usually, initially, a time for performance of the contract is extended, and if the contract cannot be performed by that extended period of time, provision is made in the contract whereby both parties settle the problem of non-performance of the contract through friendly consultations. This clause also specifies the time by which the affected party will be obliged to notify the other party of the occurrence of an event included in the *force majeure* clause.

5.3.19 Language

The language in which the technical information is to be rendered must be specified, as must the language for correspondence between the parties.

5.3.20 The Period of Validity of the Contract

The duration of the contract must be determined by specifying the date on which the manufacture of the product will commence. The licensee must ensure that approval of all governmental authorities is obtained by that date.

5.3.21 Termination of the Contract

In this clause provision is often made for its early termination by notice. It is further mentioned that upon the expiration of the contract, the obligation to supply materials by the licensor during the period of validity thereof, including the right to the patents of the licensor in force at the date of termination of the contract, must remain until the date on which the patents lapse.

This clause also provides that in the event of bankruptcy or liquidation of either party or assignment in favour of creditors of either parties, the other party may terminate the contract by written notice in sufficient time. Also, upon a breach of a fundamental term of the contract by either party, the contract will come to an end, and the affected party will have the right to bring an action in breach of the contract, and seek damages.

5.3.22 Settlement of Disputes

In most cases, provision is made for conciliation and arbitration for settling disputes that may arise under the Agreement. In the event of referring a dispute to arbitration, the parties should state how many arbitrators will constitute the tribunal, and the location at which the arbitration will be held.

Although in most cases, the law of the host country (the law of the licensor's country) is chosen as the governing law for settling disputes, it is suggested that provision should be made for the application of general principles of law recognised by states as the governing law, as a choice of the host country's law or of the home country's law, often provokes controversy, and in the circumstances if an award is rendered its enforcement may not be assured.

Furthermore, the location of the arbitration should be a country other than the country of the licensor or of the licensee. It is also suggested that the choice of the procedural law and substantive law should coincide, otherwise there will be conflict between the procedural law and substantive law. Details of arbitration should be included in an Annex.

5.3.23 *Effectiveness of the Contract*

In this clause a number of issues are mentioned:

(i) it is stated that the Agreement will be signed by the authorised representatives of both parties, usually in the country of the licensee, and that both parties will have the Agreement ratified by their respective Governments;
(ii) whether the Agreement may be cancelled within the first six months after it has come into force;
(iii) the date on which the Agreement will come into force and the period for which it will remain valid;
(iv) the continuing liability of debtors must be met after the Agreement comes to an end;
(v) the language of the Agreement is stated;
(vi) any amendment to the terms of the Agreement must be agreed to by both parties and incorporated into the original Agreement upon signature of both parties.

5.4   Conclusions

Although certain terms are commonly used in all transfer of technology contracts, depending upon the nature of technology and the laws of the countries of transferor and transferee, additional terms may have to be included. Furthermore, in drafting such contracts, the laws of the country of the licensee are to be followed very rigidly. The parties must also ensure that the contract is valid and enforceable under the laws of the licensee's country.

6 Project Finance

6.1 Introduction

Generally speaking, project financing stands for raising finance for a project. Project financing may relate to a private project or a project in which a government or a government-sponsored body may be involved. A project involving a government or a government-sponsored body entails raising finance from international financial institutions, such as the World Bank Group or the European Bank for Reconstruction and Development or other such institutions, and in that event, the recommended practice of such institutions is required to be followed.

This chapter is concerned with the technique of raising finance in respect of private projects and some of the important legal issues pertaining to project finance. Some aspects of project financing share common elements with syndicated loan arrangements, but it is thought appropriate to discuss project financing in a separate chapter as it has own features and a negotiator is required to be familiar with them. Furthermore, a general idea of project financing should help any negotiator to prepare himself/herself for raising finance for a project particularly when a borrower lacks assets and the lenders will have to rely on the projected returns that may be generated from the project on which the loan is sought, and the security for the lenders is the assets of the project. Often assurances are provided by managers, sponsors, purchasers and of course by the host country so that there should not be any difficulty in servicing the loan. It must be emphasised however that support from the host country offers the best assurances for the lenders. In this respect one may draw analogies with the system of project financing by the International Finance Corporation under the World Bank Group.

Lenders are often reluctant to undertake the entire risk; they usually expect financial support from the sponsors. In view of the large funds required by large projects, often a consortium of companies is set up for providing finance. They are usually known as sponsors. They can either set up a joint venture or a separate project company which is registered in the jurisdiction in which the project is to be carried out. Sponsors hold shares in such companies or ventures. Most of the developing countries require such bodies to be incorporated under local law. There are however certain merits in such local incorporation: ownership in the project assets may be vested in a single company; local tax rebate holidays may be made available to the company as a local company; shares remain transferable to other parties who may wish to take over the original company; and of course, the risk remains confined to one company. The issue of having security over assets vested in a single company, rather than a joint venture, is much easier to deal with.

The popular methods of extending funds are the following:

(a) the lenders may lend to the project company and the sponsors give a completion guarantee to the lenders; or
(b) on the strength of guarantees by the sponsors the lenders advance loans to the project company up to the completion point, and with the project being operative, the project company sells the product to a buyer under a long-term contract, usually, on a take-or-pay type, and with the proceeds pays back the loan. As to sponsors, they issue a guarantee to the project company in regard to the obligations of the purchaser under the take-or-pay contract, and the project company assigns the take-or-pay contract or the benefit and the guarantee to the lenders as security.

Then, there exist off-balance sheet finance and forward-purchase financing. These are explained below.

6.1.1   Off-balance Sheet Finance

This technique is adopted when the local accounting practices allow a loan or guarantee to be shown as a trading transaction; thus the loan or guarantee will be off (outside) the balance sheet. This technique helps improve the credit standing of the borrower. Furthermore, when a party is subject to restrictions on borrowings and guarantees and the available quota has been used up, this technique may be found useful. It is to be emphasised that unless the local accounting practices allow it, this technique may not be adopted.

6.1.2   Forward Purchase Financings

As the title suggests, under this method proceeds are advanced to the project company as advance purchase price for the product. When the project comes on-stream, the project product will be sold to a third party under a take-or-pay agreement, and the income will pay back the loan. On the strength of a forward purchase agreement, sponsors issue guarantees to the project company. The ultimate credit for the finance is the guarantor of the take-or-pay contract. It is clear that if any of the links in the chain does not work, the guarantee will be adversely affected. In this method of financing, rights are assigned to various parties in the chain, and an assigned person does not become entitled to a right greater than the assignor. Furthermore, if a party in the chain experiences any adverse financial situation (insolvency, for example) all others in the chain will suffer as a result. Advance purchase price is determined on speculative prices and if the market price fails to attain the speculated level the arrangement may not work. This type of project financing therefore entails risks. Indeed, lenders often refuse to advance funds on completion risk. Sponsors are therefore required to provide a guarantee even on the issue of completion of the project by the stipulated date.

Where however the lender expressly assumes certain of the commercial risks, and agrees to advance finance, it does so under the method which is known as limited resource finance. Under this method, the lender's opportunity to recover is limited to specified proceeds or security, whether cash flow or otherwise. The cash to be realised from the profit is usually placed in a trust account. On the other hand provision may be made whereby neither the borrower nor the guarantor(s) will be obliged to repay the loan, nor will the sponsor be obliged to contribute capital when loss may result from a specified risk. When a product or material is subject to market volatility, the aforesaid parties often refuse to undertake any obligation to repay the loan against cash flow.

Depending upon the terms of finance agreed to by the parties, the clauses are incorporated into the agreement. Whereas the first part of this chapter is concerned with the general issues of project financing, legal issues pertaining to it have received attention in the second part.

6.2 Risks

This matter has been discussed in chapter 3 of this work. Traditionally, the issue of risk minimisation is considered by lenders; but there is no harm for a prospective borrower to identify the factors that should assure the prospective lenders of risk-less investments. Of course, the prospective lenders should, nevertheless, take precautionary measures against risks, usually by means of insurance policies, by examining the feasibility study critically, by taking warranties from the borrower as to the authenticity of the information provided by taking 'waivers' from a sovereign borrower, by confirming the non-application of foreign exchange regulations prevalent in the country so as to facilitate remittances of funds, and by making a contractual obligation to include the loan repayment provision in the national budget, in addition to treating the loan as a national loan. This last procedure is possible when government support for the project is received.

As stated in the chapter on syndicated loan arrangements, a borrower should also respect the 'reporting conditions' in any borrowing arrangement whereby an early warning system often helps avert defaults in repayments. Many of the issues and clauses which have been discussed in relation to syndicated loan arrangements are relevant to this chapter too; therefore in many cases, cross-references have been made between these two chapters. Most countries, developed and developing, have adopted investment legislation; lenders should study the relevant legislation, in addition to studying the foreign exchange regulations prevalent in the country. Defaults in repayment of loans are often attributable to the lack of a critical study of the risks to which a prospective borrower may be prone. A genuine borrower has also a duty to minimise risks in borrowing.

6.3 Third Party Undertakings

Third party undertakings obviously shift some of the risks relating to project finance from the lenders to third parties. It is useful and necessary to identify the techniques of minimising risks for the lenders. Depending upon the nature of the project, third party undertakings may vary. Nevertheless, it is possible to identify some of the third party undertakings common to most manufacturing plants.

6.3.1 Advance Payments from Customers

A proper feasibility study should identify the capability of prospective customers, based on market research. Definite contracts of purchase from the borrower, when the plant will commence production, often allow the borrower to take part payment in advance. Such an arrangement becomes very reassuring for the prospective lenders. Advance payments operate as working capital loans.

6.3.2 Completion Guarantees

Completion guarantees assure the prospective lenders of repayment of the loan. Completion guarantees must be provided not only by the prospective borrower but also by the sponsors of the project. These guarantees must be realistic, that is, given the resources, human or otherwise, and other conditions such as climate, supply of materials, etc., the project can be completed by the date by which the borrower plans to complete. Completion guarantees are particularly important in respect of construction projects. Lenders are required to study the issue of completion guarantees from a practical and realistic point of view. Any prolongation of the completion schedule simply entails additional finance and adjustment to the other schedules. Prospective lenders should therefore examine whether the financial plan contains any built-in provision for additional expenditures for such situations. Completion guarantees form part of the project sponsor's responsibility, but any delay in completion may present a risk of default for the lenders; hence prospective lenders should study this issue seriously.

An effective completion guarantee entails certain important elements. Strictly speaking, failure to complete a project should not be regarded as an event of default, but the lenders' prospect of recovering funds may be jeopardised. Therefore, they should seek a guarantee from the sponsor of the project to the effect that if failure to complete the project by the stipulated date is treated as a ground for default in repayment by the borrower, the sponsor will remain liable for repayment of the loan. Of course, failure to complete by the original schedule will create a problem with the customers who have made advance payments for products. Where there is more than one sponsor, each sponsor must remain liable severally but not jointly.

Sponsors should be required to deposit an agreed amount with a bank acting as trustee to open a letter of credit in favour of the lenders or to give a promissory note in the same amount to allow the lenders to enforce it in the event of any default by the borrower. Sponsors often raise additional finance from the lenders to meet the additional expenditures or negotiate with the lenders an extended schedule for repayment.

The other risks which may be responsible for the project being incomplete and the probable protection thereto have been discussed in chapter 3 of this work.

6.3.3 Working Capital Guarantees

Under such guarantees, the sponsor is required to give an undertaking to maintain adequate working capital in the borrower's account for the period between the date of completion and the anticipated date of commencement of production. It should be pointed out that sponsors are usually reluctant to give such guarantees as they consider that their financial responsibility, as guarantors, terminates with the completion of the project. Legally speaking, it is a responsibility for sponsors towards the borrower, and not towards the lenders.

6.3.4 Management Contracts

Lenders may require borrowers to enter into management contracts in order to ensure that the project is properly managed by experts. This issue is not usually important when the borrower belongs to a developed country. In many countries, governmental approval is necessary for arranging management contracts, whereas in the Eastern Bloc countries, a management contract forms a significant part of a project.

6.3.5 Take or Pay Contracts

These are also known as price support agreements. Under such agreements, sponsors are asked to guarantee a minimum price on the project's output. It is a risky agreement for the sponsor, as the price of the project's output may fall, but sponsors often feel obliged to agree to this term.

Take or pay contracts or price support contracts are generally used in mineral projects, and the lender may insist on them. They virtually stand for a guarantee of payments by the sponsor. The sponsor may seek some relief by entering a *force majeure* clause whereby it can avoid the obligation on the grounds of unforeseen circumstances or circumstances which were beyond its control. It must be ensured however that the *force majeure* is not drafted either too broadly or too narrowly. Lenders however often ask for assignment of proceeds as a further protection.

6.3.6 Agreements Relating to Raw Materials or Supplies

Although lenders often ask for such agreements in the form of a clause a good feasibility study should clarify this issue. Where the completion of the project is dependent upon the supply of raw materials or other goods from foreign sources, the need for such an agreement arises. A borrower should also include in the feasibility study alternative sources of supply of raw materials. This becomes a crucial issue when the relationship between the country of supply and the country of the borrower suddenly becomes strained. This clause does not serve as a guarantee, but operates usually as a reassurance for the lenders that the completion of the project by the stipulated date will not be in jeopardy. Of course, where the borrower is the provider of raw materials and other goods required for the completion of the project, it is not necessary to include this clause.

6.4   Security for Payment

This issue becomes particularly important following the completion of the project. The lenders would like to ensure that the loan is secured regularly, particularly out of the profits generated by the project. Without security, lenders will be reluctant to advance finance. In fact, without determining what might be offered as security against the borrowing, borrowers should not attempt or initiate negotiation of project finance, as it is usually secured finance.

The following are usually offered as security: mortgages over immovable property; assignment of concessions; assignments of take-or-pay contracts; insurance policies, charges over equipment, movable assets and shares of the project company. It is usual to set up a trust account to deposit the proceeds of sale of project products. At the negotiation stage, negotiators should ensure whether under the local law any of these securities may be enforced, and also whether enforcement would be cost-effective, bearing in mind that the market price of movable assets often decreases. In certain countries, charges may not be created over certain assets or properties. A correct evaluation of securities often may not be attained. A foreign lien may not be created over certain assets or properties. A correct evaluation of securities often may not be attained. A foreign lender may not be allowed *pari passu* right under the local law, and the conditions for security against international loans may be onerous. Of course, the borrower's assets in the lender's country may facilitate obtaining security over them. One of the means of ensuring avoidance of default is for the lender to have control over the project. Of course, the terms and conditions of control often become matters of controversy. Nevertheless, non-financial issues are as important as financial issues, including securities.

Attention should be paid as to how best the project may be performed, as it is the effective performance of the project that may avoid many of the risks undertaken by lenders. Effective management of the project entailing its smooth running and consequential profitability, should be the objective of the project company, as the incidence of default may thus be avoided, and the question of enforcing securities would not arise.

Repayment of loan may be secured by the following means: restrictive covenants on the borrower, mortgages and assignment of proceeds. These means are now briefly discussed.

6.4.1 Restrictive Covenants on the Borrower

By this means the borrower's freedom to allow further security on its assets and/or revenues is restricted. 'Negative pledge' is a form of restrictive covenant whereby the borrower gives a warranty that it will not attract any more security on its assets and revenues, which have already been offered to the lenders as security for the loan. Other forms of restrictive covenants are restrictions on additional debt or maintenance of specified debt-equity ratios.

Again, before a restrictive covenant is imposed, the borrower should, ideally, be required to give a 'disclosure declaration' confirming its current debt position, and the current valuation of its assets. By the same token, it should also be required to do the same in respect of its incomes.

6.4.2 Mortgages

Asking for a mortgage on the borrower's real property or sources of production seems to be a theoretical gesture for obtaining security. There exist a number of difficulties in securing a mortgage on a borrower's real property/estate or sources of production. In many countries, foreign entities are not allowed to own real property; can a mortgage actually be created on the borrower's real property?

In traditional practice, lenders, nevertheless, ask for mortgages on the borrower's real property and/or sources of production. From a practical standpoint, it may be suggested that lenders should instead ask for a 'negative pledge' or a declaration that the borrower shall not part with any of its assets without the consent of the lenders.

6.4.3 Assignment of Proceeds

This is a device whereby a borrower may be required to assign the proceeds of sales earned in hard currencies, whether in part or in full, to the lenders, so as to ensure repayment of the loan. In this way, the lenders maintain a claim on the project's revenues. Assignment is usually based on long term sales contracts.

Assignment can be effective in respect of long-term sales contracts in that a borrower may not be able to settle its debt by this means over a short period of time. There is no reason however why in appropriate cases assignment may not be prescribed over a short period of time for repayment of loans.

However, there are several important issues which must be borne in mind in adopting this device of assignment. First, in order to avoid the adverse effect of price fluctuations, the sponsor should be asked to fix a specified minimum contract price. If the world market price for that product falls below the specified minimum contract price, then the sponsor will be required to pay the difference. Second, the lenders must ensure that these long-term sales contracts are valid and indeed enforceable in the purchasers' countries or in the host country. Third, the lenders should ascertain whether the government entity or the borrower has any legal objection to assigning the proceeds of sales under such contracts to the lenders.

After the prerequisites have been satisfied an assignment is activated through a particular mechanism. The borrower (now the seller) enters into an assignment procedure with a trustee acting on behalf of the lenders on the authority of which the borrower assigns its right to the trustee to receive payments under those sales contracts. The borrower must be notified by the trustee of the location(s) of payments and each payment must be acknowledged by the trustee. The borrower is not concerned with the reason for choosing particular locations for payments, save the fact that the borrower (now the seller) is not subject to any rule or regulation prohibiting it from remitting funds to a particular jurisdiction. Lenders should also ensure that assignment of such funds is not contrary to the foreign exchange regulations in the borrower's country, and if so, whether a waiver may be allowed by the government of the borrower. Ideally, in the case of a government borrower, such assignment should be taken into account in the annual budget of the country. Assignments cannot be adjusted against counterclaims or set-offs, as the nature of liabilities under each of these heads is different, and a trustee can be appointed for assignments only.

One of the prime difficulties with the device of assignment is that in the event of a purchaser failing to pay, the assignment mechanism will come to a halt. Secondly, a successor government may not like to continue with the system of assigning proceeds of sales to a trustee; as a precautionary measure against such an eventuality, lenders should insist on their loans being recognised as a national debt for the host country (which should be possible to do if the borrower is a government department or a government-sponsored body or if the project is a government-backed project). This is how the assignment mechanism may be saved. The caution must however be entered that any government may adopt new foreign exchange regulations, in the national interest, whereby the assignment mechanism may be adversely affected or be stopped, at least for a short period; however if this does happen, provision for interest on the allocated fund must be made. Furthermore, lenders should take precautionary measures against a trustee being bankrupt, while the assignment contract remains valid.

The assignment mechanism may not be regarded as a foolproof mechanism for the collection of debts. It is to be treated as one of the mechanisms for this purpose. Furthermore, instead of depending upon the market price mechanism, which may be subject to fluctuations, a definite sum agreed upon by parties should be allocated to the assignment mechanism; this will avoid the difficulties caused by market price fluctuations, whether in the local market or in the world market.

The assignment mechanism operates in a circuit: the borrower sells to long-term purchasers, who pay the proceeds of sales to the appointed trustees, and the latter pay the money to the lenders on the basis of the assignment.

There is yet another type of agreement which is believed to offer some kind of security to lenders, namely, *through-put agreements*. Under such agreements the shipper of oil and gas undertakes to ship through the project's pipeline certain minimum quantities of oil and gas. The tariffs earned on shipments are paid towards the debt, irrespective of whether the minimum quantity of oil or gas has been shipped. Again, this method may be defeated by an enforcement of *force majeure*.

In reality, none of the security devices may be promptly enforced especially when the government of the debtor country may need to stop payments owing to a national emergency or by virtue of having a very adverse balance of payments, although suspension of payments may not be for a long period of time. Where however a genuine cause of default exists, lenders may like to activate the renegotiation clause for rescheduling the debt. This is why a renegotiation clause in loan agreement is very important, although very strict conditions must be imposed so as to ensure that this clause is activated only in the circumstances specified by the clause.

Perhaps the best kind of security may be obtained from the host country concerned in the form of undertakings that the loan will not be subject to foreign exchange regulations, that the remittances will not be prohibited and that it would be regarded as a national debt.

6.5 Inter-Lender Arrangements

Where finance is raised by a number of lenders, as in syndications, the borrower should take certain precautionary measures. What if one of the lenders fails to provide the funds on the stipulated date, and the borrower in consequence, fails to settle his debts with his subcontractors, or pay for other essential items. As stated in the chapter on Syndicated Loan Arrangements, in such cases, the syndicate remains liable to the borrower, but members of a syndicate will undertake several liability among themselves. Conversely, in the event of a default by the borrower, all lenders must agree to a common action against the default, that is, enforce the default provision in the loan agreement. The events of default clause should therefore clearly identify the events to justify default.

Provisions should be made whereby an individual lender may bring an action against the borrower on grounds of default, but no lender is allowed to take action outside an inter-lender arrangement; in other words the inter-lender arrangement must also provide for such action by an individual lender.

6.6 Some General Issues that Should be Considered in Accepting a Property as Security

Property may generally be divided into the following categories:

(a) immovables;
(b) tangible movables (equipment, goods etc.); and
(c) intangible movables (goodwill, shares, licences etc.).

The status of a security (particularly of negotiable instruments) and the law governing them vary from country to country. Some securities are ranked as floating charges.[1] This is another issue which should receive the attention of negotiators. The following are some of the important issues that negotiators should consider in accepting assets as securities.

(a) Whether the borrower's title to the property is free from encumbrances.

(b) Whether the borrower is bound by a negative pledge in respect of any security it now proposes to offer.
(c) Whether any other creditors, notably liquidators, tax authorities, lien holders etc. have any priority claim over the security proposed.
(d) Whether the security can be extended to include the property that is attached to it; for example, buildings built on a piece of land which is offered as a security; or any improvements made on an existing security; for example, technological improvements made on a vessel. Conversely, whether a charge on a property can be extended to include any after-acquired property; that is, the previous charge-holder may have a claw on other properties attached to the one that has been offered as a security.
(e) Whether the borrower will be prepared to 'top up' the security if its saleable value decreases. This provision should be discussed at the negotiation stage, and not after the value of the security has actually decreased. Of course, if the value of the security increases over a period of time, the borrower's position improves, and this possibility need not be included in the clause, as in enforcing a security, the borrower will automatically have the benefit of the appreciation in the value of the security.
(f) Where by legislation a ceiling for security secured by mortgages (land and/or ship) is fixed, care should be taken to ascertain that such a situation has not been reached, and if reached, whether security on such property may nevertheless be effected by any other valid means in that jurisdiction, perhaps by advancing the loan to a newly-formed company and claiming security on different assets.
(g) Where under the local legislation a mortgage is required to be expressed in the local currency even through the loan has been expressed in foreign currency, the risk of fluctuation in exchange rates and the consequence on the security of depreciation in the value of the local currency, must be taken into consideration. Negotiation must secure the position of the lender for the deferral that might be caused by currency fluctuations, by arranging additional security. This may be achieved either by obtaining a larger security to cover the difference that may be caused by currency fluctuations or by indexing the local currency value of the security to the appropriate rate of exchange.
(h) At the negotiation stage, it should be ascertained whether there exists any restriction on the sale, and in particular, sale by auction of the security. The reason why public auction is mentioned is that good title in the property without any encumbrances is verified prior to putting it up for public auction, which may not necessarily be the case when security is

sold through private sales; quiet liens sometimes become evident after a private sale has been effected.

(i) In the case of sale of stocks and shares, as securities, it should be ascertained whether the security holder may be required to satisfy the requirements of local securities law.

(j) There are certain other issues on which clarification should be sought: requirements for local stamp duty; enforcement of the security in foreign jurisdiction(s), if possible or necessary; requirement of governmental approval for the grant of security to a foreigner; registration formalities; permission to have proceeds repatriated; whether remittances of proceeds are subject to the local exchange control regulations; whether a waiver may be sought and whether under the local legislation, the mortgagee is required to obtain the best possible price for the secured property, when selling it.

6.7 Registration of Securities

It has become a very common practice in most jurisdictions to have a security registered when it is not in the possession of a lender. Although, registration of securities seems to offer apparent satisfaction or consolation for the lender, in effect it may create problems for it, particularly when multiple registrations are effected whether in the same jurisdiction or different jurisdictions with similar requirements. It attracts publicity. Unless the system of pervasive registration is abolished, multiple registration will add to the publicity process. Non-registration may negate the security. A negotiator is required to know the law of the country in which security is obtained. Furthermore, it is essential to ascertain whether a liquidator or any creditor has already a charge on the security. Whether liquid assets (money) obtained as security may be subject to foreign exchange regulations, and if so, whether any waiver may be obtained from the government concerned, and whether succession of the government might affect the security.

In the case of floating charges over assets situate in more than one jurisdiction, or securities in the form of negotiable instruments, which are transferable, registration presents difficulties. The registration formality in each jurisdiction must be looked into, and it must be ascertained whether it may be satisfied, and where necessary, securities may be enforced. It is not appropriate to discuss the registration system prevalent in any specific jurisdictions as it would be difficult to justify the choice of the jurisdictions.

One can write extensively on project financing; and suggest various types of precautionary measure, but the fact remains that there are certain limits to securing guarantee as to repayment or an effective enforcement of securities. *Pari passu* or negative pledge for example may offer some degree of satisfaction; but where the same assets have been used for multiple securities, the prospect of realising funds by enforcing them becomes remote. Furthermore, where securities are located in the host country, enforcement may entail considerable difficulty and time, unless of course the security has been registered as a valid and a priority security. Where however guarantees are given by banks, the issue of acquisitions and mergers may present a problem in that usually the bank, the giver of a guarantee, if merged, does not give any constructive notice before the merger takes place; therefore, the beneficiary of the security does not have any means of doing anything to protect its position. The action that the beneficiary may take against the acquirer, or the former guarantor bank, is usually of a limited nature after the acquisition and merger have actually taken place. Perhaps a system should be adopted whereby the beneficiary of the security must be notified by a constructive notice of acquisition and merger.

The perennial problem remains as to the enforcement of a security when the assets are not located in the lender's jurisdiction, or when guarantee is secured from a bank and its enforcement in the local jurisdiction is subject to very stringent methods and law.

The applicable law for guarantee or security contracts often presents another problem. Usually, it is the law of the place of the guarantor that becomes the governing law, but a negotiator should be mindful of whether in the event of a dispute arising under a guarantee contract the chosen law may give it an unexpected result.

The question is not what the current commercial practice is, but how the practice may be improved. Quite often lenders experience difficulty in enforcing guarantees or securities for the reasons stated above, and in desperate situations quite often such difficulty is resolved by insurance policies. So the fact remains that enforcement of guarantees or securities still presents great difficulty and therefore a review of the practice is urgently needed.

This is not to suggest that guarantors do not honour their promissory contractual obligations; what is important to consider is whether in view of the difficulties, whether seen or unforeseen, attached to the enforcement of guarantees and securities, de-localisation of guarantees in an alternative and appropriate jurisdiction or their enforcement in the jurisdiction where assets are available and remittances of assets in hard currencies will be possible should not be made compulsory. Particular problems emanating from multiple guarantees on the same assets, where separate unencumbered assets are not available, but the realisation of the loan can nevertheless be effective, should receive the attention of the international community.

6.8 Some Important Legal Issues Pertaining to Project Finance

After the finance has been raised, a prudent negotiator should, perhaps with the help of an experienced lawyer, consider the legal issues pertaining to project finance. These issues need to be considered either because of the special status of the borrower, or because of the special features including the legal environment of the country of the borrower. For example, where the borrower is a government department or an alter ego of a government, it may be necessary to do what is known as veil-lifting in order to ensure the real legal status of the borrower. The legal implications of a sovereign borrowing should be seriously considered by a prudent negotiator.

6.8.1 The Legal Position of the Borrower in a Project Finance Agreement

Borrowers may broadly be divided into two categories: public and private. Both types of borrower have their own characteristics. A private borrower is basically a private entity, and is treated as an ordinary contracting party, unless special circumstances ascribe a special status to a private entity, such as when such an entity would seek finance from the International Finance Corporation, a component organisation of the World Bank Group. Such an entity must be sponsored by the government of the state in which it is incorporated. In project financing, a private entity, irrespective of its status and influence as an investor, must be treated as a mere private contracting party, which is subject to all types of scrutiny applicable to such entities for the purpose of assessing risks.

A public entity also presents risks, and bearing in mind its characteristics, and its involvement in rendering public services, risk studies in relation to project financing in which public entities including public sponsored entities are involved, should be carried out. The legal position of a private borrower is not difficult to determine. In addition to determining its legal personality by referring to its registration/incorporation, the value of its assets and the extent of its liabilities should be ascertained, as its business track record must be sought and analysed. In the case of a private corporate entity listed on the relevant stock exchange, it becomes easier to obtain information and assess its strengths and weaknesses. Unlisted corporate bodies are not necessarily to be rejected, and in this context one should appreciate the reason why the Alternative Market was developed as part of the London International Capital Market.

In other words, a pragmatic approach should be taken by a prospective investor in considering project financing in respect of a private corporate body. But, if the borrower is a public or sovereign party, several legal issues merit consideration. Some of these issues are considered in the subsequent sections:

(a) The legitimacy of a government and the issue of succession of the loan obligations The problem really relates to the issue of the recognition of governments rather than the recognition of states. Once a state is created and is known as a state, the problem ends there, particularly when it has identified by the international community as a state. For example, statehood of North Vietnam or Taiwan has never been questioned by anybody; but it is the issue of the recognition of the governments of these countries, for whatever reasons, that has become a point of controversy. In fact, most of the members of the United Nations have not recognised the governments of North Vietnam and Taiwan. In the context of this chapter, the question arises, what is the status of these governments in relation to project financing by other governments? In other words, what would be the important legal aspects of project financing when a government is unrecognised or when a successor government is recognised? Of course, this issue is now particularly relevant to newly born states, but the answer may be found in the practice established by the Western states in this regard. Take, for example, the Tinoco episode.[2] While ruling Costa Rica as a dictator, Tinoco granted concessions to certain British companies and issued bank notes. After deposing Tinoco, the new government declared those concessions and bank notes invalid. The dispute was referred to a sole arbitrator whose award confirmed that Tinoco's acts in this regard were binding upon the successor government irrespective of whether Tinoco's government was regarded as unconstitutional under Costa Rican law and recognised by many foreign governments, including the government of Great Britain which was a claimant in that case. This award confirmed that national debts are passed to successor governments provided they are regarded as such. In other words, in lending funds to a government, the lender should provide for succession of obligations as national debts in the loan agreement.

In recent years, the rationale of the award seems to have been followed by the Claims Tribunals in the claims brought by claimants against the new regime of Iran in respect of the loans attracted by the regime of the Islamic Republic of Iran.[3] Alternatively, there is no reason why finance borrowed by governments may not be regarded as national debt[4] as governments represent the state. The issue of whether a government was despotic or not is immaterial.

Furthermore, where the fiscal autonomy of a state survives, even after the total extinction of that state, the debtor-creditor relationship still subsists, and the liability of the debtor remains unextinguished. It must be emphasised however that the lending of funds to unrecognised governments is always risky for two primary reasons: (a) commercial dealings with such governments may after time be regarded by such governments as an indirect or implicit act of recognition by the other government; and (b) from a legal standpoint, the status of the loan agreements remains a controversial issue, that is, in the event of a dispute arising under such agreements, resolution of that dispute may prove to be difficult.

The question of state succession should also be considered in relation to unification, division and creation of territories by cession.[5] In each of these situations the legal position of the borrower changes and an amendment to the loan agreement to that effect becomes necessary. Upon unification of a territory, the previous foreign territory's loan obligations must be taken over by the government of the unified territory; and a reverse procedure and effect takes place when a territory is divided or a new state is created by cession; if the plant, for example, on which a loan was allowed now comes under the newly born state, then the obligations under the loan agreement must be undertaken by the government of that state, and the loan agreement must be amended accordingly. Such issues must be discussed by the two governments before the division of the territory takes place or a new territory is created by cession, and amortisation of the loan must be negotiated.[6] Loan agreements with governments thus have a unique status in law. If they were treated as ordinary commercial contracts, then the principle of succession would not have applied to them; on the other hand, loan agreements may not be regarded as treaties, particularly when one of the parties is a non-governmental entity, as parties to a treaty are usually states. Vedross thus described such instruments as instruments of a *sui generis* character.[7] Of course, for the reasons stated above, loan agreements, for example, concluded between the International Bank for Reconstruction and Development and one of its member states do not present any problem as to the application of the principle of succession. They are, in practice, treated as treaties, which are capable of binding successor governments. From an academic standpoint, the sanctity of the principle of *pacta sunt servanda* in regard to such agreements must be respected by the successor debtor(s). In cases where it was economically possible, the debts of all colonial territories which attained their independence after 1945 (the decolonisation period) followed the territories themselves.[8] Economic realities are often taken into account in settling war debts too.[9] Loan agreements with governments assume a unique status in international law, and the principle of international responsibility applies to them.

(b) Sovereign immunity According to the principle of sovereign immunity, a sovereign and/or its *alter ego* is immune from the jurisdiction of another sovereign; this principle, in theory, is based on another principle of international law, namely the principle of sovereign equality. It would be inappropriate to go into the details of the reality or unreality of the principle of sovereign equality in the context of this work, nor would it be advisable to elaborate on this principle in the context of loan agreements; suffice it to say that this principle may not be applied to loan agreements to which a sovereign or its *alter ego* is a party.

Briefly, two other sub-principles need to be explained in relation to the principle of sovereign immunity: *jure impeii* and *jure gestionis*, which distinction was found necessary by certain states, namely, Belgium and Italy.

In fact, the principle of *jure gestionis*, which allows immunity only in a restrictive fashion, have been long applied by countries, namely, Austria, Egypt, France, Federal Republic of Germany (now Germany), Greece and Switzerland. On the other hand, the principle of absolute immunity was ardently followed by the United Kingdom and the United States until just over two decades ago. The rational for the application of the principle of absolute immunity even when a sovereign or a sovereign entity would be involved in commercial matters was first established by Marshall, C.J. in *The Schooner Exchange v. McFadden*[10] case, in which he stated inter alia, that:

> One sovereign being in no respect amenable to another, and being bound by obligations of the highest character not to degrade the dignity of his nation, by placing himself or its sovereign rights within the jurisdiction of another can be supposed to enter a foreign territory only under an express licence, or in the confidence that the immunities belonging to his independent sovereign state, though not expressly stipulated, are reserved by implication, and will be extended to him.

The principle of sovereign equality may be the basis for allowing absolute immunity to a sovereign, but apparently for commercial reasons, the principle was extended to include the commercial activities of sovereigns too. While according to certain authors, the law on sovereign immunity, whether in its absolute or restrictive form, is uncertain,[11] according to others, the principle of absolute immunity represents the law.[12] Yet again, certain authors consider any distinction between sovereign and non-sovereign acts of a state unsustainable,[13] as a sovereign state does not cease to be a sovereign entity when it is engaged in a commercial activity. This view is in conformity with the views maintained by the proponents of the state-controlled economies.

The controversy about the basis for maintaining any distinction between *jure imperii* and *jure gestionis* is never-ending. According to Weiss, the nature of the act should be the determinant.[14] This rationale was, in effect, maintained by the court in the *Trendtex Trading Corporation v. Central Bank of Nigeria*.[15] In *Congreso del Partido*,[16] the House of Lords conclusively decided that the purpose of the act is of no significance. Of course, controversy may always arise as to the classification of activities as commercial or non-commercial unless an entity is proved to be an alter ego of a state or government department, which issue may only be settled by the government concerned.[17]

It is to be emphasised however that the sovereign immunity principle is universally recognised; waiver of immunity in respect of commercial activities of a sovereign may only be sought as an exception to the principle, and provisions for such exceptions may be made by statutes.

The US Federal Sovereign Immunities Act, 1976, made exceptions to the jurisdictional immunity of a foreign state by stating, inter alia, that:

> A foreign state shall not be immune from the jurisdiction of courts of the United States or of the states in any case-
>
> in which the foreign state has waived its immunity either explicitly or by implication, notwithstanding any withdrawal of the waiver which the foreign state may purport to effect except in accordance with the terms of the waiver.
>
> in which the action is based upon a commercial activity carried on in the United States by the foreign state, or upon an act performed in the United States in connection with a commercial activity of the foreign state elsewhere, or upon an act outside the territory of the United States in connection with a commercial activity of the foreign state elsewhere and that act causes a direct effect in the United States.[18]

The State Immunity Act, 1978 (U.K.) provides that:

(a) A State is not immune as respects proceedings in respect of which it has submitted to the jurisdiction of the courts of the United Kingdom.[19]

(b) A State is not immune as respects proceedings relating to a commercial transaction entered into by the State; or an obligation of the State which by virtue of a contract (whether a commercial transaction or not) falls to be performed wholly or partly in the United Kingdom.[20]

The principle of *jure imperii* which has a legal justification is extended to include the principle of reciprocity between states. 'The practice of the English Courts until the State Immunity Act, 1978 came into force was based on the principle of sovereign equality of which the principle of *jure imperii* is part. It is also worth considering whether the support for the principle of *jure imperii* even when a sovereign was involved in commercial activities was not based on economic reasons; such support would also promote trade and investment on a bilateral basis (reciprocity). On the other hand, the issue of *jure imperii* and *jure gestionis* is subject to two opposable controversies: (a) whether from a legal standpoint, a sovereign's status may change when it may be involved in a commercial activity for the state; and (b) if *jure imperii* is rigidly applied then a large number of state-controlled economies will automatically be entitled to this privilege and will not be amenable to foreign courts even when they may be in breach of their contractual obligations arising under commercial contracts.[21] The application of the principle of *jure gestionis* seems to have an economic and financial basis rather than a legal one. In fact, the distinction between *jure imperii* and *jure gestionis* is artificial and legally unsustainable.

(c) Exceptions to the principle of Sovereign Immunity Waiver of immunity by an express act (whether by means of a treaty or a contract or by statute) is an acknowledged means of invoking exceptions to the principle of sovereign immunity. Examples of implied waiver are available however, albeit in limited state practice.[22] Immunity is not available where proceedings relate to the acquisition by a foreign state, whether by succession or as a gift of movable or immovable property subject to the jurisdiction of the forum state.[23]

Based on decided cases[24] and the considered views of academics,[25] it seems that no immunity may be allowed where proceedings relate to rights or interests in or use of immovable property of which the defendant state is the owner or possessor or in which it has or claims to have an interest. The location of the immovable property gives the jurisdiction-forum *rei sitae*. In fact, if the *forum rei sitae* lacks jurisdiction, no other jurisdiction in such cases may assume jurisdiction.

The validity of claims for immunity by component states of federations still proves controversial,[26] but it may be safe to state that unless a component state has been allowed total authority over financial matters, and operates an authorised agent of the principal (the federal authority), logic does not allow such an entity to claim immunity; the principal must waive immunity. Incidentally, in the past, municipal courts extended immunity to various state agencies;[27] but in view of the US Federal Sovereign Immunities Act, 1976, and the State Immunity Act, 1978 (U.K.) it is doubtful whether the courts of these two states would now do so, when involved in commercial activities. The decision of the Court of Appeal in *Trendtex Trading Corporation v. Central Bank of Nigeria*, in which the government of Nigeria had substantial control, but was denied sovereign immunity because of its involvement in a commercial activity, confirms the view that central banks under substantial governmental control may not be regarded as organs or agents of government, and allowed immunity.[28]

The European Convention on State Immunity, 1972[29] also adopted the doctrine of restrictive sovereign immunity in respect of commercial transactions. The domestic legislation of the following countries, for example, has also embodied the doctrine of restrictive sovereign immunity; Australia,[30] Canada,[31] Singapore[32] and South Africa.[33] It should be pointed out however that the incorporation of the restrictive immunity doctrine in the domestic legislation of a state may not automatically assure a lender that sovereign immunity may not be claimed as such legislation may be subject to various judicial interpretations.

(d) Limits to the application of Sovereign Immunity Application of the doctrine of sovereign immunity may be limited to certain special cases: (i) it is successfully pleaded that there is no nexus between the transaction and the forum in which the action is and (ii) when the execution may be limited only to the assets linked to the transaction.

(e) The issue of characterisation of a transaction Characterisation of a transaction as a commercial transaction, whether by judicial pronouncements or otherwise, may not necessarily exempt the transaction from the privilege of sovereign immunity. In *Callejo v. Bancomer*,[34] despite the transaction being characterised as a commercial one, the court rendered its decision on the propriety of the application of the act of state doctrine.[35]

Furthermore, characterisation of a transaction as a commercial transaction and the seeking of a judgment for actual execution against the assets of foreign state or a public body are two different issues: although under the Swiss judicial practice, loans contracted foreign sovereigns are not to be subjected to sovereign immunity, the courts decline to assume jurisdiction in relation to execution of a judgment against the assets of a foreign state unless the transaction has some connection with the Swiss territory.[36] The element of territorial connection of a transaction in respect of such matters has also become evident in the US Federal Sovereign Immunities Act, as the Act is applicable to commercial acts only if they are carried out in the United States or if they maintain a substantial connection with the United States.[37]

Although the 1988 amendment to the US Federal Sovereign Immunities Act (sub-paragraph 6 to section 1610 (a)) removed the requirement of nexus for execution of arbitral awards against all commercial assets of an award-debtor, under section 1610(c) and (d) of the same Act, pre-judgment attachment for the purpose of acquiring jurisdiction is not possible.[38] Both pre-judgment and post-judgment execution may be available in France, Germany and Switzerland in very limited circumstances.[39]

There are two other issues which should also be considered in relation to the execution of a judgment on a commercial transaction in which a sovereign entity may be involved, on assets held by that authority: (a) whether immunity from suit is different from immunity from execution of a judgment; and (b) when the available assets for levying execution are meant for mixed purposes (that is, both commercial and non-commercial purposes). As to (a) one may consider the decision of the English Court of Appeal in *Alcom Limited v. Republic of Colombia.*[40] In this case, although the court designated the contractual transaction to which the Republic of Colombia was a party, as a 'commercial transaction' to which immunity would not be allowed, the assets held by the Colombian authorities were beyond the reach of the English Jurisdiction as they were meant for governmental purposes, which issue was already confirmed by the Colombian sovereign authorities. Incidentally, whether such assets are meant for sovereign purposes or not is to be confirmed by the sovereign authority concerned, and not by anyone else. Neither a pre-judgment nor a post-judgment attachment to the assets of a foreign sovereign or sovereign entity is possible under the U.K. State Immunity Act.

As to (b), no clear-cut answer seems to exist. Whereas in *British Shipping Co. v. Republic of Tanzania,*[41] the US court ordered an attachment on mixed accounts justifying that such an act came under the provision of the Federal Sovereign Immunities Act, in *Liberia Eastern Timber Corporation v. Republic of Liberia,*[42] the US courts allowed mixed accounts immunity.

Jurisdictional restrictions and the legal problems pertaining to the characterisation of commercial transactions may defeat the purposes of seeking and obtaining waiver of immunity. Perhaps the international commercial world should consider why a uniform practice may not be developed in this regard, even by way of exceptions to the principles – domestic legislation which should also be applicable to pre-judgment and post-judgment execution of judicial orders.

By the same token, it may be pointed out that perhaps project finance agreements should not be subject to any domestic law, and that there is no reason why these agreements may not be governed by a neutral law, such as the general principles of law recognised by states, and disputes arising under them may not be settled at a neutral forum at which a neutral procedural law should be applied.

6.9 Conclusions

Finance may be raised from capital markets (usually in the form of syndicated loan arrangements on the Eurobond market) or from international institutions, such as the World Bank Group. What is known as project finance in the commercial world, under the World Bank system is known as project cycle. Of the three institutions under the World Bank for this purpose, the International Bank for Reconstruction and Development and the International Development Association follow a standard project cycle, and the third institution, the International Finance Corporation has its own standard project cycle system. [43] This chapter concentrates on private project financing, although it must be pointed out that mixed financing (private and international institutional) is also possible. Incidentally, regional development banks have also developed their own project financing system.

For a comprehensive idea of project financing in the private sector, this chapter should be read with the chapters on syndicated loan arrangements and the section on feasibility studies in chapter 3.

Project financing always entails risks; risk-minimisation is therefore one of the crucial issues that deserves the serious attention of the prospective lenders. One of the best securities for lenders might be by ensuring that the private project on which funding is sought has received governmental support, in addition to seeking warranties from the government of the host country, as explained above.

On the other hand, in project financing much emphasis is given to the issue of repayment of the loan, which is admittedly an important issue, but attention should also be paid to the issue which would protect a borrower's position too. Furthermore, borrowers should also be encouraged to accelerate their loan repayments process by providing for 'bullet' and 'balloon' payments. Sufficient provision should be made for remedies against defaults in payments by lenders.

As stated earlier, the most effective way of avoiding default on either side would be to activate the 'advance warning system'. Responsibility towards each other should be the main basis for lending and borrowing; indeed, responsible behaviour by both parties should protect both parties' interests in this business.

Notes

1 This is an equitable charge on the assets for the time being of a going concern. It is called 'floating' as it attaches to the assets charged in the varying conditions they happen to be in from time to time. A floating charge becomes a specific charge when a receiver is appointed or possession is taken of any property or asset comprised in the charge.
2 See the *Arbitration Report* 1923 1 UNRIAA 369.
3 See *SEDCO Inc. v. Iranian Oil Co. and the Islamic Republic of Iran*, Iran–US Claims Tribunal, Awards of 24 October 1985, 27 March 1986 and 2 July 1987, 84 International Law Reports, 484 (1985; see also *Mobil Oil Iran Inc. and Others v. Government of the Islamic Republic of Iran and National Iranian Oil Co. (Award* No. 311-74/76/81/150-3), 86 *International Law Reports* 231 (1991).
4 See further *Kleihs v. Republic of Austria*, Ann, Digest (1948), Case No. 18; see also *Doss v. Secretary of State for India* in Council (1875) CR19.
5 See the Vienna Convention on Succession of States in Respect of Treaties, 1978.
6 *Chile v. France* (The Guano Case), UN Report, vol. XV at 77.
7 A. Vedross, 'Quasi-international Agreements and International Economic Transactions', 18 *Year Book of International Affairs* (1964), 230–47.
8 See the Peace Treaty with Italy 1947, *UNTS*, vol. 49, 126; see also the case of Buacha Cmd. 7360.
9 See H. Cohen, 'The Responsibility of the Successor State for War Debts', 44 *American Journal of International Law* (1950), 477.
10 (1812) 7 Cranch 116.
11 Sir G. Fitzmaurice, 14 BYIL (1933) 117; J. Brierly, *Law of Nations*, Oxford, Clarendon Press (6th edition), 250.
12 P. Lalive, 84 *Hague Recueil* (1913 – III), 251; Oppenlieim (1) 270, Lauterpacht, 28 *BYIL* (1951), 225–6.
13 Fitzmaurice, *BYJL* (1933), 121.
14 *Hague Recueil* (1923), 525–49; 11 *ICLQ* (1962), 840; 27 *MLR* (1964), 81; *AJIL* (1965), 654.
15 1977 Q.B. 529.
16 1981 3 WLR 329.

94 Negotiating Techniques in International Commercial Contracts

17 See also the decision of the Constitutional Court of the German Federal Republic, Mann, 27 *MLR* (1964), 81.
18 S. 1605.
19 S. 2(1).
20 S. 3(1).
21 See further Lauterpacht, 28 *BYIL* (1954), 245–6.
22 See the Italian Courts' decisions in *Storelli v. Governor della Republica Francesse*, Ann. Digest 2 (1923–4), No. 66; *Hungarian R.R. v. Onori, International Law Reports* 23 (1956), 203.
23 See *Harvard Research*, 26 *MIL*, 1932 Supp. 544–72; Fairman, 22 *AJIL* (1928), 568–9, see also Brownlie.
24 Republic of Italy Case, *International Law Reports* (1951), No. 523; Republic of Latvia, *International Law Reports* (1953), 180; *International Law Reports* (1957), 221; *Sultan of Jahore v. Abubakar* (1952), A.C. 318.
25 Article 9 of *Harvard Research*; Cheshire, *Private Internationa Law* (7th edition), p. 97.
26 See further *Harvard Research*, op. cit., Article 10; Firman, op. cit., *AJIL* (1928), 568–91.
27 *Bacus SRL v. Servicio Nacional del Trigo* 1957 1 Q.B. 438; *Compania Mercantil Argentina v. United States Shipping Board* (1914) 131 LT 388; *Krajina v. Tass Agency* 1949 2 AllER 274.
28 Incidentally, bilateral treaties often provide for waivers of jurisdictional immunities in case of commercial activities. The commercial activities of state-owned vessels are subjected to the jurisdictions of foreign courts by the Brussels Convention for the Unification of Certain Rules Relating to the Immunity of State-owned Vessels of 1926 (176 LNTS 199); state enterprises are subject to the rules of the Warsaw Convention for the Unification of Certain Rules Relating to International Carriage by Air, 1929, with no reservation concerning immunity (137 INTS 11).
29 *Reprinted in 11 International Legal Materials* (1972) 470.
30 Foreign Sovereign Immunity Act, 1985, reprinted in 25 *International Legal Materials* (1986) 715.
31 State Immunity Act, 1982, reprinted in 21 *International Legal Materials* (1982), 798.
32 See U.N. Document entitled *Materials on Jurisdictional Immunities of States and their Property*, ST/LEG/SER.3/20-1982.
33 Ibid.
34 764 F.2d. (5th Cir. 1985) reprinted in 24 *International Legal Materials* (1985), 1050.
35 See also *Banco Creditor Agricol de Cartago Barke v. Bancomer* 762 F.2d.222 (2d Cir. 1985) reprinted in 24 *International Legal Materials* (1985), 1047.
36 See Judgment of 18 March 1930 TF RO 56 I 237, reprinted in 20 *International Legal Materials* (1985) 151; see also Lalive, 'Swiss Law and Practice in relation to Measures of Execution against the Property of a Foreign State', 10 *Netherlands Year Book of International Law* (1979) 153.
37 28 USC S 1603(e) 1982.
38 Post-judgment execution is however possible against the assets of a state provided the claim arose out of the transaction to which the assets relate. See further C. Chatterjee, ' Procedural Aspects of Project Finance', 10 *Journal of International Banking Law* (1993) 421–5.
39 In France, a link must exist between the commercial property on which execution is to be levied, and the loan out of which the claim has arisen; in Germany, a clear characterisation

of the property as a commercial property is essential; and in Switzerland, the loan must be connected to the Swiss territory.
40 1984 2 All E.R. 6.
41 507 F. Supp. 311 (DDC 1980).
42 659 F. Supp. 606 (DDC 1987).
43 See C. Chaterjee 'The World Bank' in *International Economic Law and Developing States: An Introduction*, H. Fox (ed.), London, The British Institute of International and Comparative Law (1992), 119–45.

7 Negotiation of Syndicated Loan Agreements

7.1 Introduction

Although the origins of syndicated loan arrangements may be traced as far back as the eighteenth century, it was only in the 1970s that they became very popular because of the circumstances of the time. The oil price-ridden economies looked for finance to correct their budget deficits, and the large amounts they sought for the purpose could predominantly be provided by syndications. During the 1980s however, the overheated economies, particularly in the West, and the easy-term loans promoted by banks in the West provided finance to many, particularly the developing countries, through the same arrangements. Interestingly enough, no identifiable pattern of syndicated loan agreements has emerged although certain clauses seem to be included, as a matter of course in most of such agreements.

It is the purpose of this chapter to identify such clauses in order to give negotiators an idea of what they should negotiate, bearing in mind that the purposes of a syndicated loan may require additional clauses in particular circumstances. It must be emphasised that in a syndicated loan arrangement, a borrower's interest and purposes cannot be ignored. The purposes of a syndicated loan arrangement are predominantly two: (a) to assist a borrower to raise funds for meeting the expenses of a project; and (b) to ensure that the lenders also earn profits in the form of interest.

7.2 The Initiation of a Syndication

It is usually through contacts that syndicated loans are arranged. The prospective borrower contacts a bank with which it has had business relations, and that bank will contact other probable banks to persuade them to join the proposed syndication. The first bank is known as the lead bank. Any proposal for a syndicated loan requires to be supported by a very detailed feasibility study – that is, of the project for which funds are to be raised. This feasibility study must contain information on the basis of which the prospective lenders may decide whether or not to advance the loan. This document is also known as the dossier. Syndicated loans are quite often sought by governments. It is for the syndication to study the risks that it may run in advancing a loan to a project, whether governmental or non-governmental.

It is appropriate to maintain that it is for the borrower to make its case viable for an offer of a loan. The prospective borrower is also required to assure the prospective lenders of the minimum risks that may exist in advancing the loan. In fact, it should not prove difficult to obtain information on the matter from other sources. The more information that a prospective borrower provides, the easier it becomes for the lead bank to convince the other prospective lenders to consider the proposal in a positive manner. The lead bank is also a party to the syndicate, and hence it also acts as a lender.

7.3   The Negotiation Process

Negotiation of syndicated loans is a serious matter from the initial stage, as the question of risk looms large for the participants in a syndicate. Most of the negotiation process is concerned with assessment of the risks. An honest disclosure of all material facts by the prospective borrower is therefore sought by the prospective lenders. Indeed, the lenders require the prospective borrower to give them a warranty as to the validity of the statements made by the prospective borrower. Although a warranty in such a case is a unilateral document, it carries full legal effect and it is an enforceable document. In other words, if at a later date, default in payments occurs, which may be attributed to nondisclosure of certain material facts, a disclosure of which would have prompted the lenders to decide against the loan, the borrower will be held liable in misleading the lenders.

Risks in lending always become one of the most important focal points. In the case of a government borrower there exists the perception that the government will either default or delay in making payments or that the government might change resulting in uncertainty of payments. This perception is unfounded as the debt is usually treated as a national debt, and the successor government in the event of a change of government, remains obliged to service the loan.[1]

But what would be the legal position when the debtor loses the territory in which the project was being built and/or under operation, after completion?

In such a situation, the original debtor remains liable, but from a practical standpoint, the state that has gained the territory with the project must be regarded as the successor of the debt. The lenders should therefore make a provision to this effect in the loan agreement, so that a new agreement with the successor state may be concluded, and the amortisation of the debt must be done.[2]

The question of security is however important in respect of all syndicated loans. A prospective borrower should therefore come to the negotiating table with definitive and sustainable answers on these issues.

Prospective lenders would also like to know whether the investment for which money would be lent will be utilised in the most profitable manner so that the investment becomes a source of income for the borrower, which, in turn, would help it service the loan.

If the loan is sought on a project which would generate income, such as a bridge over a river, then the prospective borrower should be prepared with a positive and viable answer as to how it will service the loan. The prospective borrower should also have its strategies ready as to how it intends to spend the fund, and whether it has adequate resources, human or otherwise, to realise the project. The life of a project is also another major issue in considering an application for a loan.

A sovereign borrower is often required to waive its immunity in concluding a loan contract. In a syndicated loan arrangement, both parties, the borrower and the lenders, must stand in the same legal position.

As for lenders, there are certain important issues that they should consider during the negotiation process. The first issue is the risks involved in lending the money. The feasibility study on the project on which the loan is sought provides the basis for ascertaining risks. Furthermore, the general political climate, and economic conditions in the country help in studying risks. Second is the current position of the proposed borrower as a debtor; whether the proposed borrower is already burdened with unpaid debts, and if so, the extent to which it is burdened. In the event of the proposed borrower being burdened with other debts, whether the syndicate will have a priority position as a lender; in other words, whether the *pari passu* rule will apply. Third, the issue of security is an important one. Fourth is the issue of succession of the government and/or cession of territory. Public international rules are clear on this last issue in that in the event of a government being replaced, the successor government remains responsible for the debts of the predecessor.[3] By cession, however, the territorial boundaries of the state of the government borrower may change, and if the project on which the loan has been allowed now comes under the territorial jurisdiction of a new sovereign, the latter is required to service the loan. Clauses covering these two issues should be included in a syndicated loan agreement. Fifth is whether the country has a history of natural disasters. Sixth issue is whether the government has a history of default in paying debts. The seventh issue covers the environmental risks that the project might present. Although this point may seem rather far-fetched, there are cases to establish that lenders have been accused of lending funds for projects that have polluted the environment. Incidentally, the World Bank has a policy whereby no funds may be allowed to any project which is not environmentally sound.

It is not possible to exhaust the list of issues that lenders and borrowers should consider and negotiate in regard to a proposal for a syndicated loan. Which issues should be considered very much depends upon the nature of the project and the international standing of the prospective borrower.

7.4 Organisation of Syndicated Loans

The prospective borrower is required to give the lead manager (the lead bank) a mandate on the basis of which it initiates discussion with the prospective lenders. The primary function of the mandate is to develop a relationship between the prospective borrower and the prospective syndicate. In other words, on the basis of the mandate, the lead manager works for both the borrower and the syndicate. The mandate also identifies the parameters of the lead manager's functions. The lead manager is normally required to send a memorandum of information which contains details on the borrower's financial position and other relevant information, e.g. some basic information on the project on which the loan is sought. The lead manager must also mention to the prospective lenders whether the prospective borrower is a government entity or a government-sponsored entity. Whether a memorandum of information constitutes a regulated prospectus depends upon the legislation in the relevant jurisdiction; however, the local legislation may require one of the following to be satisfied: (a) if the memorandum is treated as a prospectus, certain information according to the law of the jurisdiction must be included in it; and (b) registration of the memorandum may be necessary, whether with a securities commission, a registrar of companies or another authority prescribed by law.

Securities legislation is not applicable to such memoranda of information when one of the following grounds exists:

(a) if the syndication does not constitute a public invitation;
(b) if the borrower is a government or government-sponsored institution; and
(c) if participation in the loan agreement is not construed as 'securities' and 'debentures' under the local securities legislation.

After the prospective lenders have confirmed their willingness to consider lending the funds, the lead manager will communicate to the borrower on what terms and conditions the loan may be allowed. It is at this point that both parties should seek legal advice for scrutiny of the draft loan agreement. Legal experts must have sufficient experience in syndicated contract negotiations, but the fact remains that the basic terms and conditions will be determined by the parties concerned. The primary function of lawyers is to incorporate the terms and conditions in a formulated and uncomplicated fashion.

Before identifying the clauses that should be included in a syndicated loan agreement, it would be appropriate to discuss briefly the duties and roles of a lead manager and an agent.

7.5 The Lead Manager

It has already been explained that the lead manager who is appointed by a prospective borrower, must act for both parties as the 'link man' and submit the dossier on the prospective borrower and the project so that at the negotiation stage the prospective lenders are not required to speculate on any fundamental issue. At the initial stage, the lead manager should also notify the prospective borrower of any questions that the prospective lenders have raised in respect of the loan application. The prospective borrower should be able to supply the information prior to holding the negotiation. The lead manager's role relates mainly to the following: sourcing, structuring, selling and servicing. It must be concerned with these four main and related issues. Through the lead manager, both parties can have issues clarified. It is the lead manager who also acts as the mediator when necessary, and tries to ensure that no misunderstanding whether on the part of the prospective borrower or of the lenders interrupts the negotiation.

It must be pointed out however that a lead manager may not be held liable for any misleading information given to it by a prospective borrower, although it may be held liable in negligence for any act in which it failed to exercise 'due care' and 'skill'. In order to protect its position, a lead manager should seek a warranty from the prospective borrower in which the borrower must undertake that whatever information it may provide to the lead manager in connection with the loan application is correct and not in any way misleading.

If the prospective borrower accepts the offer made by the prospective lenders, the lead manager will negotiate the loan agreement with the borrower in accordance with the terms settled by the prospective lenders. A draft agreement is forwarded by the lead manager to the participants for their comments and approval. Each of the participants may seek separate legal advice on the draft agreement and put forward proposals for amendments, if any, before the loan agreement is finalised. Each participant bank remains responsible severally; the lead manager must therefore ensure that the extent of liability of each participant has been clearly identified and the lead manager is required to give each participant a participation certificate denoting the extent of its participation.

Where however the lead manager becomes the only lending bank, in theory, with the funds provided by other participants of the syndicate, the other participants must undertake contractual obligations with the lead manager as to their obligations on a regular basis, and what action may be taken in the event of a default on their part. The lead manager will undertake to pay *pro rata* share of the receipts from the borrower.

The relationship between the participants in a syndicate often remains undefined; however, the possible forms are: novation, assignment, joint venture, trust etc. In fact, in the interest of the borrower, the relationship between the participants should be clearly defined; otherwise, in the event of a default on the part of a participant in providing finance by a stipulated date, the borrower may have to seek legal remedies against the syndicate and individual participant although, in practice, the entire syndicate remains liable to provide the missing funds. It should be pointed out that it is not obligatory to appoint a lead manager, although there are clear advantages in doing so.

7.6   The Agent

After a loan agreement has been concluded, an agent (usually another participant bank) is required to collect the monies from the participants in order to forward them to the borrower on a specified date. This duty of an agent is important in that it must have the monies from the participants on a date mutually agreed upon, so that the fund may be transferred to the borrower's bank on a scheduled date. Any failure in this regard must be treated as a default in and breach of contractual obligations on the part of participants, and the borrower can bring an action on default and breach of contract. It is to be appreciated that the borrower may arrange payments to many parties on the basis of the anticipated funds from the participants on a specified date. Incidentally, an agent cannot disburse funds unless the borrower has served a withdrawal notice for each withdrawal. This may be done by an arrangement with the borrower's bank, but from a legal standpoint, the actual service of withdrawal notices is essential, as, in the absence of such notices, the lenders may be given the impression that the borrower would not require any more funds. The agent bank is required to keep the participants (lenders) informed of the receipt of the withdrawal notice from the borrower, and the participants are required to transmit their funds to the agent. An agent must also keep records of all transactions (receipts from participants and disbursements to the borrower) and determine the amount of interest on the loan and collect it. An agent must not disburse any fund unless it is satisfied that the documents it received from the lead bank are genuine and correctly completed; in other words, the agent bank is responsible for checking the documents; it may be held liable in negligence for failing to check documents with due care and skill. In practice, the lead bank is often appointed the agent bank, and in that event, the lead manager performs the duties of an agent bank.

An agent must not delegate the authority imposed on it, as a person who undertakes a delegated duty has no authority to delegate, in turn, to any sub-agent. In fact, a clause delimiting the authority of an agent is usually incorporated in syndicated loan agreements. Furthermore, its duties and liabilities are also required to be delimited, for example, if an agent goes into liquidation after receiving the funds from the participants, but before disbursing them to the borrower (although the timing between these two stages is rather short), then the agent must remain liable for the loan to the borrower, and in the event of its causing delay in disbursing funds to the borrower, the agent will be required to pay interest too. Conversely a similar situation can arise after the borrower has paid back an instalment into the agent's bank account. Payments made by a borrower to the agent bank (and if the lead bank is the agent bank, a separate account must be opened for receipts and withdrawals) amount to payments to the syndicate. In order to protect the position of the syndication receipts are paid into a separate account in the name of the agent, and held in trust for the participants; therefore, a separate clause to this effect is included in the loan agreement.

The extent of liability of an agent may be limited by incorporating certain special clauses, such as a claw back or exculpation clause. If an agent bank has paid the borrower in advance, that is, prior to its receiving funds from the participant banks, the agent bank will have recourse to the participants for the amount paid for by it, through a claw back clause; through an exculpation clause, an agent may limit its liability by providing in this clause, inter alia, that its duties are primarily of an administrative nature, and that it may not be held liable for any default, but it remains responsible for gross negligence and failure to exercise due care and skill in checking documents prior to its disbursing the funds to the borrower. An agent bank is also a participant bank or the lead bank. Depending upon the number of capacities in which an agent bank functions, its scope of duties and liabilities increases. A default in payment by an agent bank is a default against which the borrower may seek legal remedies. One of the important duties of an agent bank is to notify the other participant banks and the borrower, as the case may be, in the event of a default.

An agent bank has the right to resign as an agent bank; on the other hand, an agent bank may be asked by other participant banks, on sustainable grounds, to resign. If other participant banks lose confidence in an agent bank, it is advisable for the agent bank to resign.

A successor agent bank must be appointed by the participants immediately. It must however be pointed out that the precise nature of liability of an agent bank in a syndicated loan arrangement has not been clearly defined, although it is believed that the general rules of the law of agency may be applied in dealing with many of the issues relating to an agent bank in a syndicated loan agreement.

7.7 Offer and Acceptance of a Syndicated Loan

The formalities of offer and acceptance of a loan must be satisfied before concluding a syndicated loan agreement. The following items are usually included in an offer of loan made to a prospective borrower: the total amount of the loan, the period over which the loan must be drawn, conditions of repayment, rate of interest (if it is a loan arrangement on the Eurobond market, usually the interest rates are shown in a LIBOR – London Inter-Bank Offer Rates), agency fee, management fee, commitment fee (the consideration for the undertaking by the participants to make the amount available to the borrower from the date of signing of the agreement to the date on which the amount is disbursed), expenses, including expenses in connection with the preparation of documents and legal advice, tax and the nature of the other clauses which will be included in the loan agreement. The offer is kept open for a specified period of time. The attention of the prospective borrower is drawn to the fact that the terms and conditions of the loan will remain valid only under the existing political and economic conditions prevailing in the country of the prospective borrower. The formal offer made gives the prospective borrower another opportunity to consider whether or not to accept the loan. If an offer is accepted by the prospective borrower, the lead manager will start syndicating the loan.

By making an offer and by communicating acceptance of the offer, the lead manager consolidates its position as well as the position of the prospective borrower and the lenders. Offer and acceptance form the bases of the contract.

7.8 Some of the Most Important Clauses that are Included in Syndicated Loan Agreements

It is to be re-emphasised that in most cases one of the parties is a sovereign state or a public-owned entity and the other is a syndicate. The presence of a government or a government-sponsored entity does not change the commercial character of the loan agreement, and it is treated as a commercial agreement. A combination of private law and public law issues may be required to be considered in drafting a syndicated loan agreement. However, below is a list of clauses which should be included in a syndicated loan agreement. It must be pointed out that this list is not an exhaustive or exclusive one; the terms and clauses may vary according to the terms of negotiation. The list below simply gives an idea of the important clauses that should be included in such a loan agreement.

7.8.1 The Preamble

A preamble details the purpose of a loan. Its importance lies in the fact that in the event of the loan agreement, parties and the court or tribunal may refer to it for verification of whether or not the parties have acted in accordance with the prime purposes of the agreement.

7.8.2 The Definition Clause

This clause includes the definitions of certain important terms which may be referred to in interpreting the loan agreement. Some such terms are: advance, availability data, fixed rate, interest payment date, LIBOR, prime rate, currency of loan, withdrawal, termination date(s), business day etc. It is for the parties to include such other terms as they may find useful in connection with their specific agreement.

7.8.3 Conditions Precedent

This clause denotes the conditions that a borrower required to satisfy before any amount is disbursed by syndicate. Usually, a confirmation is required from borrower that it has full power and authority to execute and deliver the loan agreement and to perform and observe provisions. It is for a syndicate to impose any conditions; whether a condition is acceptable or not must be confirmed by the prospective borrower in sufficient time.

7.8.4 Conditions of Repayment

The duration of repayment must be fixed by the parties; however, usually it varies between six and 12 years, unless both parties have arranged for a 'bullet' or 'balloon' repayment (in the latter case, the amount of repayment increases gradually, although the rate of interest may remain constant). Usually, again, no repayment of capital is required during the first few years of the loan. In the event of a borrower having failed to repay the capital by the stipulated date, the agent has the authority to instruct the borrower to repay the entire amount of the loan immediately, particularly when the loan is unsecured. This is also another reason that the lenders should examine the feasibility study very carefully, and where possible, ask for securities.

7.8.5 Disbursement Clause

By virtue of this clause, which is addressed to the lenders, the agent bank advises the participants of the amount which each of them must make available by a specified date. This clause also includes the consequences of default on the part of the syndicate. Usually, if any participant fails to provide its share of the fund available by the specified date, the other participants of the syndicate give an undertaking to provide that amount. This clause also includes an undertaking indicating the joint and several liabilities of the participants in respect of making funds available by the specified dates.

7.8.6 Fees and Interest

Fees usually include the administrative or management fee. In the current practice, commitment fee is excluded. Interest rates are usually governed by the prime rates, that is, the applicable rate for prime customers in the United States or by LIBOR, the latter being generally used in respect of Euro-currency loans.

Depending upon the nature of risks of non-repayment, a margin is established for each loan. A borrower is therefore required to pay interest either according to prime rate or LIBOR, in addition to the margin established. It should be noted that for the purposes of calculating interest, 360 days constitute a year on the LIBOR market. Failure to pay interest may lead to capitalisation of the amount, or a syndicate may exercise its right whereby it may ask the borrower to repay the entire amount of the loan immediately.

7.8.7 Events of Default

This clause includes those situations in which a default in payment may be declared, and the borrower may be required to make payment of the loan earlier than the stipulated date. Events of default primarily fall into two categories:

(i) default occasioned by non-repayment by the borrower; and
(ii) other events of default.

Whereas actual default allows the lenders to take action under the loan agreement, other events of default provide lenders with an early warning system, which may prompt lenders to investigate the causes of potential default by the borrower. Such an early warning system helps the lenders to initiate a renegotiation of the terms of the loan, where appropriate.

7.8.8 Covenants

Under this clause the borrower is warranted not to create encumbrances on the loan whether in the form of mortgages or charges on its assets or to notify the syndication as soon as it becomes aware of a situation that might lead to a default in payment. It is for the parties to agree upon the issues that should be included in a covenant. However, the following clauses are usually included in a covenant: budget, maintenance of government approval, *pari passu*, and reporting. These are briefly explained below.

Budget Where a borrower is a government entity, the government concerned will be required to have the repayments approved by the authorities concerned as an item of the country's budget.

Maintenance of government approval Under this clause, it is for the borrower to ensure that governmental legislation, such as that restricting the release of foreign exchange or repayments is not applied. They shall be immune from any governmental restrictions prohibiting or restricting repayment of the loan in the stipulated foreign currency.

Pari passu This clause ensures that the lenders will be at par with other lenders from which the borrower has raised finance. In the case of private borrowers, *pari passu* remains intact even when the borrower's management changes, but the lenders will however be required to be notified of any changes having an effect on the loan. In the case of government borrowers, however, the *pari passu* covenant does not automatically bind the successor government (if there occurs a change of government during the tenure of the loan agreement), but generally, in order to maintain their credibility, governments undertake the predecessor's obligation in this regard.

Reporting Under this clause, a borrower is required to report certain information to the syndicate on a regular basis. For example, in the case of a government borrower, it is usually required to report on the general trend of the economy, trading position, balance of payments position etc., whereas a private borrower would be required to supply profit and loss accounts, quarterly reports on turnovers etc. It must however be emphasised that a syndicate maintains its right to seek any information from the borrower at any time to ensure that the repayments will be made.

7.8.9 Miscellaneous

In this clause are normally included those items which may not be incorporated in any other clause, such as amendments, costs and expenses, right of set-off, consent to jurisdiction, waiver of immunity, governing law etc.

7.9 Conclusions

It is not possible to discuss all the possible important headings and subheadings of a syndicated loan agreement in one chapter. Depending upon the terms and conditions of a loan, the clauses may vary. The discussion in section 7.8 simply attempts to explain the meanings and contents of some of the important clauses common to most syndicated loan agreements. Below are some of the subheadings which are usually included in a syndicated loan agreement.

This subheading usually includes: the credit facility, commitment availability, calculation of the amount of the advances, notice to banks of borrowing, conditions of borrowing, making the advances. Currency of payments, manner of payment, sharing of payment, insufficient funds, funds incorrectly disbursed, charging of accounts, taxes. Conditions precedent to the first availability date, conditions precedent to each subsequent availability date, notice of default. Affirmative covenants of the borrower, negative covenants of the borrower, instruction of the borrower. As stated earlier, these headings and subheadings can never be exhaustive. Standard definitions of terms and standard clauses are usually followed by drafters of syndicated loan agreements.

Notes

1 See *SEDCO Inc. v. Iranian Oil Co. and the Islamic Republic of Iran*, Iran-US Claims Tribunal, Awards of 24 October 1985, 27 March 1986 and 2 July 1987, 84 *International Law Reports* 484 (1991); see also *Mobil Oil Iran Inc. and Others v. Government of the Islamic Republic of Iran and National Iranian Oil Co.* (Award No. 311–74/76/81/150-3), 86 *International Law Reports* 231 (1991).
2 See *Chile v. France* (The Guano Case), U.N. Report. Vol. XV, at 77.
3 See footnote 1.

8 Negotiation of International Construction Contracts

8.1 Introduction

In view of the fact that a series of subcontracts is involved in an international construction project, the expression 'international construction contract' is a misnomer. The so-called international construction contracts are those contracts in respect of which contractors perform their work outside their home countries. These contracts may take one of two forms: (a) contracts to design and supervise construction; and (b) construction management. Under the former type, the employer (a government or a private entity) may decide to have the design work done by its own company or by an architect or engineer. Design work includes preparation of the plans, designs and specifications of equipment. After completion of the design work, the construction work is entrusted to a different company, which is usually elected by means of a tender. It is usual for a contractor to procure equipment and materials for the project, although the architect or engineer may also procure them on behalf of the employer. However, under this form, the principal function of the architect or engineer is to supervise the work of the contractor who carries out his work with the help of other people in the chain. The following subcontracts are usually involved in this form:

(a) contract between the employer and the engineer or architect;
(b) contract between the employer and the contractor; and
(c) subcontracts between the contractor and suppliers of materials or construction firms.

Under the second form, the employer engages a firm which coordinates the work of the contractors (the main contractor and the subcontractors). The main contractor remains accountable to the management firm, i.e., the construction manager. This is usually known as the construction management approach to a project. The construction manager may be responsible for the design and preparation of specifications of the project; otherwise this task is entrusted to an architect or engineer. The construction manager usually reviews the designs, drawings and specifications, advises on the project schedule, assists in selecting subcontractors and coordinates their work, but he/it must not direct their work. Thus, the construction management company may not be held responsible for any failure of any subcontractor in carrying out its duties, nor may it be responsible for the method(s) applied by the contractor(s) for the construction of the work. It simply takes a supervisory role, and is in no way involved in the technical aspect of the project. The following contracts are usually involved in this form:

(a) contract between the employer and the construction manager;
(b) contract between the employer and engineer or architect;
(c) contracts between the employer and contractor(s); and
(d) contracts between contractor(s) and subcontractors.

It is therefore crucially important to determine what form these contracts should take. Irrespective of the difficulties involved in defining an international construction contract, the fact remains that these contracts (or the combinations of contract) must describe the work, the respective obligations of each party and other essential elements.

8.2   Preparation for Negotiation of an International Construction Contract

Construction contracts are complex in nature. They require very thorough negotiations. In planning such a contract, an employer should select a team of people who possess knowledge and experience in this field of activity. Such teams should consist of a project manager, engineers, management experts, an accountant and a lawyer. Many may not support the idea of including a construction lawyer in the team, but in order to ensure that contracts are properly drafted the participation of a lawyer from the initial stage proves to be useful.

The primary functions of the team will be: to determine the basic method of constructing the project, management of the project, financing of the project and the method of contracting the project.

The employer should have a clear idea of the following: the type of works he plans, the time period by which the works must be completed, the projected costs, the sources of finance, the types of contractor he requires, the purpose of the project, his role whether as a manager or otherwise, the local laws and regulations relevant to the works including laws and regulations of procurement and import and export. In fact, the employer should have a blueprint of the works prepared in advance, to be able to negotiate the terms properly and effectively.

The employer should also know what type of construction contract he would like to negotiate: whether a full turn-key or a semi-turn-key or a contract to design or a construction management contract.

The term 'turn-key' is significant in that it stands for a type of contract which when completed will allow the employer to turn the key to the industry, that is, it becomes a fully operational programme. A full turn-key contract necessarily requires the contractor to undertake full responsibility for designing, constructing and commissioning works in order to complete the programme. The employer signs a contract with one contractor, which is usually a company or a consortium of companies, authorising the contractor to deal with all other aspects of a programme, such as engineering, specifications of equipment, construction, supply of machinery and equipment and training of the labour force, in addition to taking additional responsibility for the technical management of the project both during its actual operation and after completion.

Although entrusting a project in its entirety to one firm of contractors has its own advantages in that the contractor through its expertise would be able to provide all material and engage other subcontractors for a speedy conclusion, there does exist the risk of total failure by the contractor. Therefore, a prudent employer should foresee and calculate the risks by studying the track record of the contractor, and if necessary, entrust certain aspects of the project to other firms, which will be required to coordinate with the principal contractor.

Under a semi-turn-key contract, the employer engages a firm of contractors for the design, procurement and completion of a section of the project, and the remainder of the work is done by the employer itself. Depending upon the capacity and expertise of an employer, the agenda for negotiation of an international construction contract varies.

8.3 How Should an Employer Select a Construction Contractor?

There are usually two methods of selecting construction contractors by an employer: (a) by tender; and (b) by a sole source.

8.3.1 By Tender

Under this method, an employer seeks to obtain contractors by making what is known as 'invitation to tender'. Prior to its placing any 'invitation to tender' usually in popular newspapers or by a more selective method, an employer must prepare certain documents pertaining to the project, and an invitation to tender package usually contains the following:

(i) basic drawing of the work;
(ii) specifications of the work/design;
(iii) schedules of rates;
(iv) conditions of the construction work;
(v) instruction to tenderers; and
(vi) the requirement of bonds, whether performance or tender or bank guarantees.

An employer must ensure that the information supplied by it in these documents is accurate, and not misleading, as in the event of any information being found inaccurate or misleading, the acceptor of a tender will have ground to bring an action in negligence and misrepresentation of facts. Irrespective of whether an employer is a government department or a state-owned body or a private body, the tender package should be as detailed as possible.

An 'invitation to tender' should also specify the following:

(i) the date by which the tender must be submitted;
(ii) the amount and form of any tender bond/guarantee;
(iii) the number of copies of documents to be submitted;
(iv) a clear statement that the employer may not necessarily accept the lowest bid; or that the employer retains its right to reject all bids and publish a new invitation to tender; and
(v) the tenderers should be asked to sign the tender acceptance form and make reservations to any conditions of the contract, if necessary.

It is for the employer to select the contractor(s); where necessary it can ask any proposed contractor to clarify certain issues.

8.3.2 Sole Source

Under the single source selection system, the employer selects and negotiates

Negotiation of International Construction Contracts 113

with a particular contractor, which is known to itself. This system has its own disadvantages in that mere familiarity may prompt the employer to negotiate with a single contractor, but it has the advantage of maintaining confidentiality, that is, the employer need not publicise the project.

8.4 Is There any Standard Form of International Construction Contract?

There does not exist any universally accepted standard form of construction contract, although there exist certain standard conditions which are often included in international construction contracts. Standard forms are developed and adopted by various associations of engineers, contractors and architects. The UN Economic Commission for Europe has published various contract forms for the supply, construction and supervision of plant and machinery. The UN Federation of Civil Engineering Contractors and the US Institute of Architects have also developed standard forms of construction contract. The standard form of construction contract developed by the UK Federation of Civil Engineering Contractors is widely used. The standard forms of contract which are most often used in international contracts are: Conditions of Contract (International) for Works of Civil Engineering Construction (FIDIC Civil Works); and Conditions of Contract (International) for Electrical and Mechanical Works (Including Erection on Site) (FIDIC E & M). These forms have been devised by the *Federation Internationale des Ingenieurs-Conseils* (FIDIC) and are popularly known as FIDIC forms. Under both the FIDIC forms, an engineer supervises the construction work, but whereas under a FIDIC (E & M) form the responsibility for preparing the design and specifications of the works is undertaken by the contractor, under a FIDIC (Civil Works) form the contractor is not required to undertake any such responsibility; in other words, FIDIC (Civil Works) separates design from construction aspects of a project, but FIDIC (E & M) takes a unified approach. Revised versions of forms have already been published by FIDIC.

8.5 Some of the Most Important Clauses in International Construction Contracts

As stated earlier, various standard forms have been adopted by various institutions; nevertheless it is possible to identify certain common clauses in most of the international construction contracts. In this section, the contents of such clauses are summarised; however, it must be pointed out that, in practice, parties follow one of the established standard forms. The purpose of this Section is to discuss some of the important issues that should be considered in connection with the clauses described below.

8.5.1 Preamble

This clause states the principal objectives of the project stressing that both parties have, in good faith, concluded this contract. Many agreements do not contain this clause, but its inclusion is significant in that in order to justify any departure from the primary objective of the contract, courts/tribunals often rely upon this clause.

8.5.2 Definitions

As with all other contracts, the definition clause in an international construction contract should include the definitions of the key terms used in the contract, including the related documents – terms such as project, employer, works, subcontract works, plant, site(s), materials, suppliers, commencement date, date of completion, and any other term that the parties may find important to include in this clause for avoiding confusion during the life of the contract.

8.5.3 Project Management

The extent of authority and responsibility of all parties should be detailed in this clause. The hierarchy of authority should be identified, as should the allocation of work. The management of a project has two broad aspects: (i) management by allocation of duties; and (ii) management by supervision. It is important that the contractor expressly stipulates that it will provide all construction management and personnel required for supervision. The contractor is therefore required to specify a time period by which it will appoint a supervisor/superintendent on site. The nature of accountability between the contractor and employer, including its frequency, should also be specified. The employer specifies that it will have its representative on site; the scope of duty of such a representative should also be identified. Where the employer decides to utilise the service of an outside consultant, the scope of functions and authority of such a person must also be detailed. The outside consultant must always be allowed to work as an independent consultant to give his/her findings on the quality of the work, not necessarily solely representing the interest of the employer. Ideally, under this clause, the authority of the consultant engineer should be clearly defined as it may be very useful when decisions are necessary on issues on which the employer and the contractors clash.

8.5.4 Commencement Date

The commencement date is important in that this is the date on which the work for the project must commence. A project may not be commenced unless certain procedures have been completed by the parties. Where the implementation of a project is dependent upon the availability of finance, whether by an international organisation or by a government, approval must be received prior to specifying the commencement date. The commencement date has a bearing upon the price also. If this date is too far away, then a margin for inflation may have to be allowed. It is therefore advisable for parties to ensure that they will be absolutely ready for commencement of the work, prior to fixing the date. Failure to commence the work by the stipulated date will amount to a breach of the contract. Parties should negotiate the commencement date very carefully.

8.5.5 Obligations of the Employer

The obligations of an employer are relatively easier to identify; nevertheless, they must be detailed in the contract. The following are the principal obligations of an employer: to give unencumbered access to the site, to provide the site with all licences necessary for building the plant or machinery on the site(s), to identify the site(s) accurately, including their boundaries, to appoint its representative on the site(s), to assist in securing clearance through custom in respect of any goods, articles etc., required to be imported from abroad, to obtain local government authorisations, where necessary, and of course to pay the contract price in accordance with the terms of the contract. Provision should also be made for supplying all facilities to the contractor, whenever reasonable requests to that effect may be made by the contractor; this is because the employer may otherwise be held liable in not allowing the contractor to complete the contract project. The employer should also undertake the obligation to facilitate remittances of payments by the foreign contractor to its jurisdiction, that is, by seeking permission of the central bank, in advance, where necessary. The obligations under a contract are of a varied nature; mention has been made only of the most important ones.

8.5.5.1 Design and detailed engineering Where the contractor designs and engineers the project, it is for it to describe the plans, design, drawings, data and other technical aspects of the project. The kind of data and other information that must be supplied by the employer must also be included in this clause. If the contractor cannot rely on these data, what would be the obligations of the employer must be mentioned. In the event of one party providing incorrect information, it must bear the costs of correcting the errors. Usually, where information provided to the contractor seems to be incorrect, the contractor will be responsible for correcting this, but it will not be required to bear the costs of so doing.

It is also necessary to clarify whether drawings become the property of the contractor or of the employer, and in the latter event whether the employer may have a licence to use them. The schedule of planning, engineering etc. must be determined; and the procedure for seeking the approval of the employer or its consultant must also be identified. In order to avoid delay occasioned by the failure of the employer and/or its consultant to review and approve the plans and drawings submitted to it, in good time, a specific time schedule should be entered whereby the employer and/or its consultant will be required to signify its approval or disapproval by that time. A contractor should not proceed with the project until it has received the approval of its employer and/or consultant.

8.5.5.2 Supply of equipment and materials It is usual for the contractor to procure equipment and material, and to store them. The contract should include specifications as to the type of equipment and materials, usually in the form of an annex. The clause must also state whether the employer may have any say on the selection of the supplier. Governmental regulations may prohibit an employer from procuring materials directly or through its contractor or agent from specific suppliers. The clause should also state whether the employer or its consultant will have the right to test the equipment and/or material before they are shipped to the place of work. Usually, employers engage a separate firm to examine equipment and material at its cost. If the contractor undertakes such responsibility, a clear statement to that effect must be included in this clause. It should also be clearly stated whose duty it would be to examine goods upon arrival at the place of storage.

8.5.5.3 Construction The contractor has three principal functions to perform in relation to construction and erection of a project: to complete civil works, to erect the building, and to integrate the equipment into the project so that the project runs effectively. This clause therefore includes the issues relating to these aspects of the contractor's functions.

It is for the contractor to fix the hours of work, including the schedule and details of work; personnel, including their accommodation arrangements and local subcontractors. The employer may impose a condition whereby it will retain the right to oppose the selection of subcontractors.

The employer retains the right to examine the works on site and the contractor may be required to redo the work if not approved by the employer or its consultant. The time for redoing the work should be fixed, but if any work is to be redone because of the employer's new demand, the costs must be borne by the employer. But if a work is not tested by the employer by the stipulated time, the contractor will usually have the right to proceed, as the work will be deemed approved. Provision should be made whereby the employer will be required to give its reasons in writing for rejecting the work done by the contractor. If the contractor fails or refuses to correct the defective work, the employer retains the right to intervene and correct it.

8.5.5.4 Commencement and training The contractor must ensure that the project is fully operational. The provision of supervision, whether by a specialist or by the contractor itself, should be included in the clause. Often, the contractor is required to train the employer's staff so as to enable them to operate the plant after completion. In fact, the obligation to train the local staff normally continues for the contractor after the employer takes over the plant. Usually, the training programme is set out in the Annex to the contract, but the contractor often enters a waiver to the effect that even after completion of the training programme it should not be held responsible for their competence particularly when the trainees are not selected by it. The contractor receives remuneration for imparting training to the local people.

8.5.6   Price and Terms of Payment

Pricing of an international construction contract is a complex issue in that there exist many formulae for fixing the price; furthermore, it also depends upon the nature and scope of work a contractor and an employer may undertake. Usually, prices for project management, design, engineering and equipment are settled on a lump sum basis, and prices for other matters may be settled on a cost plus target basis or a cost plus fixed price basis. However, in fixing the price, the currency of payment must be identified as the conversion rate from one currency to another has a bearing upon pricing. Usually, payments are made in two currencies – whereas payment is made in the local currency for local expenses, the contractor's fee and the expenses incurred in purchasing equipment and material and securing labour from abroad are usually made in a predetermined foreign currency. In order to avoid losses occasioned by fluctuations of currencies, it is advisable to have the price fixed at a particular rate of exchange or to take precautionary measures against this risk whether by insurance policies or otherwise.

Payments are normally made in instalments or by advance payments or by payments based on progress or by retention payments. As in many other contracts, advance payment is a common phenomenon in executing international construction contracts. Advances (usually between 5 per cent and 20 per cent) are secured by guarantees, which take various forms, and are set-off against payments. Likewise, the practice of including a provisional sum in the contract is also commonplace when the parties are not certain of the actual costs of the project, particularly in the absence of estimates on subcontractors' work. This sum, upon estimation of all the costs in due course, becomes the 'fixed' or 'prime' cost. Payments based on progress are necessary to maintain the impetus of the contractor. Such payments are made by the employer upon examination of the work done. The schedule for such payments is usually fixed at the negotiation stage. This system has an indirect effect on the progress of work too, that is, unless the work is done to the satisfaction of the employer, payment will not be made.

Retention of payment works as a safety valve for the employer in that a percentage of the contract price (usually 5 per cent to 10 per cent) is retained by the employer from the payment as security in order to ensure that the contractor reaches its target of work. It is released upon successful completion of sections of work. Retention of payments gives the employer the advantage of being able to draw from the retained amount in the event of a contractor causing any damage to the employer by the former's non-performance of any element of the contract.

The pricing formulae are as varied as there are contracts. Nevertheless, it is possible to identify certain general pricing formulae adopted in international construction contracts.

8.5.6.1 Lump sum Under this formula, the contractor agrees to accept a fixed price for the completion of the project, and here it takes the risk of extra expenditures, unless the contract provides otherwise. In fact, a contractor should protect its position by providing for extra expenditures which prove to be inevitable owing to reasons beyond its control.

8.5.6.2 Unit price Under this formula, the contractor fixes a price for each item to be used in the works, and reaches an agreement with the employer. These are prefixed prices, and the amount is paid on each actually used.

8.5.6.3 Cost plus target price As the expression suggests, under this formula, the contractor sets a target price for the work, and the employer pays the actual costs incurred, usually on a unit price basis. If the actual costs exceed or are lower than the target price, then the excess or saving is shared by the employer and contractor.

8.5.6.4 Cost plus fixed fee Here, the contractor seeks costs actually incurred on the project, in addition to a fixed fee. This is a safe pricing system in that the contractor will justify actual costs incurred on the project by documentary evidence, are in addition it will receive the mutually agreed fee.

It must be emphasised that price and terms of payment admit of a variety of terms and flexibility based on the agreement between an employer and a contractor. Furthermore, the availability of finance, whether from private sources or from international organisations, has a direct bearing upon settling the terms of payment.

8.5.7 Schedules of Works

The importance of a schedule of works in international construction contracts can hardly be overemphasised. A schedule of works not only contains a breakdown of target dates by which the various stages of the programme should be completed, but also the date on which the employer will take over the programme at the end of the guarantee period.

A schedule of works may be amended at a later date by mutual consent of the employer and the contractor, but at the time of negotiation a schedule must be discussed, and its final version must be attached to the contract in the form of an annex. In relation to international construction contracts, there seems to exist a perception that schedules of work are not binding; it must be emphasised that schedules form an integral part of the contract; therefore, provisions in schedules must be treated as legally binding. Alterations of dates can only take place by mutual consent of the parties.

In fact, a provision should be made for renegotiation of dates of completion in the schedules of works under certain special circumstances, such as import prohibition, natural disasters, foreign exchange difficulties etc. rather than claiming a *force majeure*. It is to be appreciated that in view of the involvement of many subcontractors, it is often not possible to achieve completion of the stages in schedules of works. Undue extension of time should however be avoided.

On the other hand, an early completion of a project would also allow an employer to enjoy the benefit of the project earlier than scheduled; therefore, a provision for a bonus to the contractor as a payment in recognition of efficiency should be made in the contract.

However, provision for fixed damages (liquidated) should be made in relation to the schedule of works in case one of the parties unnecessarily delays the performance of the contract.

8.5.8   Acceptance of Works

After the project has been completed by the contractor in accordance with the terms of the contract and to the full satisfaction of the employer, the contractor must formally make over the contract to the employer, and the latter must accept it provided it is satisfied with it. Taking over can also occur in stages. The acceptance of the employer is subject to tests and standards to be achieved, details of which must be annexed to the contract.

Title and risks pass to the employer as from the date of the takeover; the employer should therefore, in consultation with the contractor, state whose personnel must carry out the tests and what raw materials must pass through the equipment, and who shall supply these materials. Minor defects may be disregarded at the test stage but they are normally included in what is known as a 'punch list' for correction at a later date.

The guarantee may still run even after the date of taking over and during the maintenance period, and after all defects have been corrected, the project will be finally examined and declared totally complete, and the performance guarantee must be released to the contractor, and the outstanding payment made to it.

The employer has an obligation to issue a certificate confirming the completion of the project and that the project is in order.

8.5.9   Amendments

Amendments may be requested either by the employer or by the contractor unless changed circumstances require them. This means that an international construction contract develops as the stages in it are completed. The programme of an international construction contract may require changes in its terms,

Negotiation of International Construction Contracts 121

which are of an operational nature. Changes in the operational aspects of a contract may have a bearing upon the schedules of works, terms of payment and even on guarantee.

What must be noticed is that changes are not self-induced, and if they are so, then the party concerned, whether it is the employer or the contractor, must bear the consequences that is, pay extra expenses.

Changes occasioned by defective work performed by a contractor are real changes, and the contract cannot be amended to accommodate them. Similarly, changes occasioned by the negligence of either of the contracting parties are to be regarded as real change: of course, a problem remains as to the prices. It is therefore advisable to provide for such situations in the form of an Annex, perhaps for extra costs for additional equipment and material or by some other formula agreed upon by both the parties. These changes in price will of course have a bearing upon the warranties. The original time schedule for the completion of the work will also be required to be modified. Provision should be made for payment of compensation to the employer for delay in completing the work. Conversely, the employer will be required to compensate the contractor when delay has been caused by the former. Delay may be excused only in the case of unforeseen events over which no party had any control but the progress of the work was in consequence, hindered.

8.5.10 Warranties

In an international construction contract, a contractor undertakes substantial obligations, and an employer seeks warranties from it. The issues on which an employer seeks warranties depend upon the nature of the obligations a contractor undertakes. Generally, an employer seeks warranties from a contractor on the following:

(i) the quality of workmanship for a specified period.
(ii) if the contractor undertakes design work, a warranty confirming that the designs will produce the results stipulated in the contract.
(iii) that the materials and equipment supplied will be the most appropriate ones for the project; it is for the contractor to secure guarantees from the subcontractors on this issue, and assign them to the employer so that the employer's position as to the product liability is secured. It is expected that the periods of the warranties relating to other matters will be longer than those of the contract period.

(iv) correction of all defects, including reduced performance caused by bad workmanship.

(v) completion date, and a predetermined amount of damages (liquidated damages) for delayed and/or inadequate performance.

It is to be noted that although an employer will normally try to have as many warranties as possible to protect its position, a competent and experienced contractor will also try to ensure that it does not give unnecessary warranties. Furthermore, most of the warranties will terminate with the completion of the work (i.e., performance of the contract). Warranties on product liability or workmanship covering a guaranteed period of the smooth running of the project normally run even after the project has been taken over by the employer.

It is also to be noticed that a contractor is not held responsible for any defect which has been contributed to by the employer. In fact, a contractor should seek a warranty from the employer on this issue.

Indeed, although there exists a general practice of certain warranties being given by a contractor, any specific warranty on any issue may be sought, where necessary, upon mutually agreed terms. A contractor usually takes out insurance policies with a view to minimising its own financial losses too. This issue has received attention in a separate section of this chapter.

8.5.11 Bonds

Contractors are required to give bonds/guarantees as to their performance. In the event of their failure to perform the contract or any of its specified obligations by the stipulated date or according to the stipulated terms, as a compensatory measure, performance bonds/guarantees are activated. Such bonds/guarantees are usually issued by banks (in the case of international construction contracts, usually for 5 per cent to 10 per cent of the contract price). As this is a complex issue, it would be appropriate to discuss briefly the various types of bond/guarantees. However, before describing them, it is appropriate to point out certain anomalies that exist in the commercial world as to these instruments. In reality, there does not exist any difference between a guarantee and an indemnity. Similarly, no distinction may be made between a counter-guarantee and a counter-indemnity. A guarantor seeks a guarantee on its guarantee, hence it is called a counter-guarantee. The idea that one bank gives a guarantee, and the other party's bank gives an indemnity against it is a misnomer; both are guarantees or both are indemnities. Guarantees are also known as bonds in the world of banking.

The principal types of bonds/guarantees are: bid or tender bonds, performance bonds, advanced payment and retention money bonds and first demand bonds. Although other bonds, such as customs bonds, equipment and completion bonds exist, this work will concentrate on the most popular ones. It is for the guarantor to determine which form of the bonds it will accept.

8.5.11.1 Bid or tender bonds These are called bid or tender bonds, because under these instruments, undertakings are given to the effect that the customer has the intention to sign the contract and comply with the terms of the contract if the tender is accepted by the buyer. A bid or tender is at the origin of such bonds, hence the title. In the event of the tender being accepted and the customer failing to proceed as planned, the beneficiary/party to whom the bond was given, will have the right to make a demand on the bond, and the bond document should include a choice to that effect. The beneficiary of the bonds does not sustain losses in that such bonds compensate the beneficiary for the additional costs that may occur in reallocation of the contract to another party. The beneficiary may of course lose time.

It is therefore, essential for any tenderer to ensure that it would be able to proceed with its own tender if accepted, otherwise, the offeror of the tender simply benefits. Usually there is no recourse to this kind of bond. It is a straightforward obligation undertaken between the offeror of the tender and the guarantor of the party that gives the bond.

Bid bonds are solely concerned with biddings. They offer protection to any increases in expenses that may be incurred by the offeror of a tender. They contain unilateral risks in that if the customer fails to proceed as planned, the offeror of the tender gains but not the party that wants to accept the offer.

Bid bonds are quite popular in the world of investment banking. Many bid bonds are offered against tenders, published by governments, semi-government and private parties, but governments and government sponsored bodies most often offer tenders on a bid bond basis. This method has been adopted in commercial practice to ensure that the parties who accept the tender are capable parties, financially or otherwise, so that only those applications that have been made by willing and able offerees are considered.

Bid bonds are normally to be given by a specific date, although in practice the period of giving such bonds is often extended by the giver of the bond unilaterally and sometimes multilaterally. One of the difficulties of giving such bonds related to the financial ability of the customer who is willing to undertake the project. One of the ways of avoiding delays in giving bid bonds would be for the bond givers to ensure beforehand that the customer is capable of performing the terms accepted by the offeror of the tender.

A bid bond is to be returned after the contract has been signed and an appropriate performance bond has been issued in favour of the party. Unsuccessful bids must be returned to the appropriate parties. In commercial practice however this practice is not strictly followed, but it is suggested that once the stage of acceptance of tender is over, a bid bond should be returned to the appropriate party to signify that it has been released from its liability.[1]

8.5.11.2 Performance bonds These bonds are given by banks in support of a customer's obligations to perform a specific contractual commitment, hence the name. For example, a foreign party may have doubts as to the ability of another foreign supplier of goods in performance of his contractual obligations but when safeguarded by a bond of performance, issued by a banker, the buyer feels assured of contractual performance under subcontracts. The buyer's position will certainly be protected when a performance bond is issued in first demand form. Such bonds are activated by buyers whenever the seller fails to meet his obligations.

Performance bonds can be of two types: first demand and conditional bonds. In the case of first demand bonds, which are in reality guarantees, the obligation to make payments arises on first demand without any proof of conditions. Naturally, these bonds are much preferred by overseas buyers. For the purpose of activating such bonds the relevant clause also provides that it must be payable on demand without proof or conditions.[2] First demand bonds are therefore conditional bonds and lawyers should ensure that in drafting bond contracts, a clause specifying 'the attribute of unconditionally is maintained'[3] is incorporated.

First demand bonds have become a common phenomenon in the international banking world and are preferred by government buyers as they would like to have the security of performance by the seller especially when a project is financed by a third party be it an international organisation or a syndication.

The obligations under first demand bonds are very difficult to ignore unless exonerated by sustainable *force majeure* clauses. These obligations are not negotiable; they are absolute in character. Conditional bonds, on the other hand, are those bonds or guarantees, the obligation under which are conditional upon the beneficiary proving default by the party who is to perform the subject matter of the bond (usually the seller or contractor). In other words, in the case of such bonds the obligation to make payment is conditional upon proving default by the party who is contractually bound to perform the subject matter of the underlying contracts. It is time consuming to enforce such bonds; naturally banks prefer first demand bonds to conditional bonds.

From a business point of view, conditional bonds are preferred by beneficiaries as they offer them opportunities to prove breach of contract for reasons beyond their control, but in the case of such bonds banks are required to specify conditions of default which will activate the bond. The legal difficulty attached to such bonds is whether the condition is sufficiently wide or narrow. In order to justify payments under conditional bonds documentary evidence of breach is normally required.

Irrespective of the type of performance bond, such bonds are normally required within a few weeks after the contract has been concluded. In practice, however, the buyer would request such bonds at the time of concluding such contracts. Performance bonds are specifically required when the other party, the seller or the contractor, is not sufficiently known to the buyer or employer. The purpose of a performance bond is similar to that of a demand bond; it may be defeated if a clause limiting the liability of the contractor or seller is allowed to be inserted in the contract, save for accepted *force majeure* grounds. There does exist a degree of conflict between buyers and sellers or between employers and contractors as to the choice of the type of bond. Whereas a buyer or employer prefers a demand bond, a seller or contractor will prefer a conditional bond.

Conditional bonds may not serve the purpose for which buyers or employers seek bonds but demand bonds may be regarded as too burdensome by sellers or contractors, as the performance of their contracted obligations may be conditional on certain factors which may be beyond their control. Although banks always prefer conditional bonds the controversy as to whether a demand or conditional bond may be sought, seems to be never-ending; perhaps the bargaining power of the parties often decides this issue.

8.5.11.3 Retention money bonds Under these bonds a percentage of each payment is withheld, until the contract has been performed and accepted by the overseas buyer or the employer, as monies are retained under the said bonds on an agreed basis. They are therefore called retention bonds. Such bonds protect the position of the overseas buyer or the employer in that it can make demand at any time whenever the seller or contractor may fail to perform its obligations.

Retention bonds can adversely affect the cash-flow position of an overseas seller or contractor, but they are the best means of ensuring that the overseas seller or contractor performs his obligations. Such bonds do not impose any extra burdens on banks as their actual liability is limited to the progress payments actually received by the overseas buyer or employer.[4]

8.5.11.4 Advance payment bonds Such bonds are common in the construction industry, as overseas employers are often required to make advance payments to enable contractors to commence works, whether principal or ancillary. The overseas employer requires bonds against advance payment, in order to safeguard his position in the event of the contractor or seller failing to carry out his obligations under the contract.

A concomitant relationship exists between the degree of the bank's liability and the extent of performance of the contractor or seller in respect of such bonds. In fact, sellers or contractors feel obliged to comply with their contractual obligations when such are issued and the bank's liability is often reduced progressively.

Advance payment bonds can be activated like demand bonds as soon as the failure to perform by the contractor or seller has been established. Such bonds should not be conditional. The overseas employer's position remains stronger than that of the contractor or seller in respect of such bonds. The overseas employer limits the degree of risk by agreeing to accept advance payment bonds, in that he makes payments in advance and he can claim on non-performance at a later date. An overseas contractor or seller may resort to impossibility of performance and this defeats the purpose of advance payment bonds. Lawyers should draft such bonds in an unconditional form.

8.5.11.5 First demand bonds When the demand is first made on a bond given by a bank this bond must be honoured, without any proof or conditions, in other words the legal obligations under such bonds are absolute and these conditions are preferred by the party that seeks such bonds. In order to maintain the absolute character of the obligation it is essential to ensure that the terms of the bond are not in any way made conditional upon anything occurring.

First demand bonds or guarantees are usually provided by banks on behalf of their customers and banks seem to prefer first demand bonds, as they enable them to steer clear of any contractual disputes that may arise under the underlying contract. A beneficiary's position under first demand bonds becomes secure and the beneficiary can proceed with the contract without much worry. If first demand bonds are multi-conditional, the purpose of securing such bonds is almost defeated because the money cannot be realised promptly. In commercial practice the phrase 'payable on demand without proof or condition' is usually included in a first demand bond contract.

Banks will not normally give such bonds unless they are absolutely certain of the financial standing of the beneficiary or their client. These bonds have no connection with nor are they in any way conditional upon any dispute that may arise under the underlying contract. In *Gulf Bank v. Mitsubishi*[5] the relevant clause headed 'Payment without Disputes' stipulated:

> Any demand made of the Bank (under) or in connection with a guarantee shall be sufficient authority to the bank for the bank's making payment of any amount so demanded and the bank need not concern itself with the propriety of any claim made or purported to be made under or in connection with such guarantee.

First demand bonds are activated as soon as a default on the part of the other party is established and a demand is made in writing. First demand bonds should be distinguished from documentary bonds. This latter type of bond can be activated on presentation of stipulated documents; otherwise their effect is similar to that of first demand bonds. Documentary bonds are in a way conditional in the sense that unless stipulated documents are produced in support of the default, the bank is not obliged to pay on such bonds. In a way, such bonds mitigate the harshness inherent in first demand bonds; only demand will do. It is to be emphasised that these bonds cannot be called conditional bonds, nor are they similar to first demand bonds.

They are triggered solely by presentation of the correct documents by the recipient.

8.5.12 Other Clauses

8.5.12.1 Termination Under this clause provision is made for the termination of the contract in the event of a material breach by a party. It also contains a list of circumstances in which the contract may be terminated. When a contract is terminated by the employer, the contractor will seek compensation at the market value of the project, up to the stage it has been completed, and compensation for demobilisation, where agreed to.

8.5.12.2 Suspension Owing to unforeseeable circumstances an employer may be required to suspend the project for a while. Provision should therefore be made to that effect in the contract. In such an event, the suspension costs incurred by the contractor must be borne by the employer; such costs usually take account of losses and inflation. Prolonged suspension may cause undue difficulty and inconvenience for both parties in continuing with the project;

therefore, provision is usually made in the contract whereby in the event of any prolonged suspension of work, either party will have the right to terminate the contract, but the contractor will still be required to be paid for the work it has already done, and the demobilisation expenses, where necessary. All warranties and performance bonds must terminate as from the date of termination of the contract.

8.5.13 Force Majeure

This is a clause which provides for the termination of a contract when an identified event takes place in consequence of which the question of continuing with the contract would not arise. Initially, the performance of the contract may be suspended for an agreed period of time, and if the normal situation does not return, or the correction of the event is not possible, then the contract will be terminated. The concept of *force majeure* originated in the civil law system; the corresponding concept in English law is frustration of contract, whereby an occurrence of an event which is not foreseeable by any party will leave the parties with no choice but to terminate the contract.

Without going into details of the legal controversy as to the scope of a *force majeure* clause, it may be pointed out that various drafts of a *force majeure* clause are available; some of these nominate events such as strikes, lockouts, civil wars as events of *force majeure*, which many lawyers may find difficult to accept. Furthermore, in so far as the FIDIC standard forms are concerned, although they contain the English law concept of 'frustration of contracts', in many cases, the governing law of the contract is a civil law, which tends to give 'frustration' the character of a *force majeure*.

Perhaps the international business community should pay attention to this issue so as to unify the practice, and rely upon 'frustration of contracts' rather than maintaining the issue of termination of a contract by activating a *force majeure* clause which admits of flexibility.

8.5.14 Language of the Contract

Where a contract is drafted in more than one language, it should be clearly stated which language will be the official language for the purposes of interpretation of its terms. In the event of a dispute arising under the contract, courts or tribunals will also use that language as the contract language.

8.5.15 Intellectual Property Rights

It is for each party to the contract to ensure that it holds intellectual property rights or has obtained necessary licences from the holders of such rights. Under this clause, each party indemnifies the other against the consequences of an infringement of these rights. In fact, this issue should be considered by the parties concerned at an early stage, but certainly prior to drafting the contract.

8.5.16 Confidentiality

In construction contracts, exchange of technical documents between the parties is a common phenomenon. Although the recipient of documents is allowed to consult their contents, it must do so only to the extent necessary for the implementation of the project, and for no other purposes and the information contained in these documents must be kept confined only to those for whom it is directly necessary to have this information. The function of the confidentiality clause is to ensure that the contents of technical documents are not divulged to third parties unnecessarily, and to provide for injunctive relief and damages in the event of a breach of the confidentiality rule.

8.5.17 Ownership

It is very important that a clause is included in the contract stipulating the date on which the ownership in the project will formally pass to the employer. It must be borne in mind that title to different items (equipment, design etc.) may pass on different dates. Passing of ownership is different from passing of risks, according to which the owner may be required to undertake the risk associated with the use of equipment long before the title or ownership in the project passes. The legal effect of passing of title to the employer is important in that it becomes the legitimate owner of the project, although certain responsibilities as to its operation may still lie with the contractor, that is, until the end of the period of warranties.

8.5.18 Waiver of Immunity

When the employer is a government or a government-sponsored entity, the contractor should ensure that the employer by means of a clause waives its immunity whereby in the event of a dispute arising under the contract, it may be brought before a court or tribunal.

8.5.19 Governing Law and Settlement of Disputes

This clause may take a variety of forms; government employers usually insist on their domestic law as the governing law of the contract, which must be applied in settling disputes that may arise under the contract. Disputes arising under an international construction contract are often referred to experts for their opinions but such opinions lack legally binding effect. International construction contracts also provide for arbitration before reputable tribunals, such as that provided by the International Chamber of Commerce or UNCITRAL (UN Commission on International Trade Law) or the London Court of International Arbitration. Care should however be taken that the procedural law and the governing law coincide; otherwise, parties that are not familiar with the procedural law of the country in which the arbitration is held may find themselves in a very uncomfortable situation. Of course, parties will have more freedom as to the constitution of a tribunal or the procedural law when they may refer their disputes to ad hoc tribunals.

Perhaps the international business community should consider whether the general principles of law recognised by states should not be applied to settle such disputes. This issue is important in that unless an award-debtor is satisfied with the award, there is no guarantee that the award will be enforced, unless an arbitration is governed by the International Convention on Settlement of Investment Disputes between States and Nationals of Other States, 1965 (ICSID). The argument should not be based on what the international business community has traditionally done. The real test is whether the traditional drafting of the governing law clauses can survive when they are put to test in the current legal environment of the international community which consists of a large variety of states having differing perceptions of their legal rights.

8.6 Conclusions

International construction contracts are very complex contracts. Although they generally follow the FIDIC and FIDIC (E & M) forms, in view of the variety of projects variations from the traditional clauses should not surprise anybody. Parties are required to know their disciplines extremely well, otherwise they may undertake obligations which they did not anticipate.

International construction contracts involve large sums of investment. Mistakes can be very expensive to rectify at a later date. In so far as a contractor is concerned, it should protect its position by taking out insurance policies, where possible; such policies may be available from governmental agencies or private institutions in its own jurisdiction.

Where finance is raised from international or intergovernmental organisations, the conditions of payment become an important issue in that in the absence of predetermined performance the availability of finance may not be assured. Risks related to international construction contracts must be considered seriously by the negotiators; most of the risks are foreseeable, hence it may be possible to take precautionary measures against them.

The success of an international construction contract very much depends upon the nature of the feasibility study that an investor has carried out; the better the study, the less the likelihood of failure.

Notes

1 G. Penn, A.M. Shea and A. Arora, *The Law and Practice of International Banking* Vol. 2, London, Sweet and Maxwell (1987), p. 263.
2 *Edward Owen Engineering Ltd v. Barclays Bank International* (1978) 1 ALL E.R. 976.
3 Williams 'on Demand and Conditional Performance Bonds' (1984) J.B.L.S.; and Arora, 'The legal position of Bonds and Performance Bond Cases' (1981) L.M.C.L.O.
4 Penn, Shea and Arora, *The Law and Practice of International Banking*, op. cit., Vol. 2.
5 2 LL.R. (1994), 149.

9 Negotiation of Petroleum Contracts

9.1 Introduction

The techniques of negotiating petroleum and mining contracts have significantly changed over the years, particularly since the period of decolonisation. These techniques became consolidated during what may be called the period of economic stabilisation of the petroleum providing countries. Such resources belong to the country in which they are found, and it has been the common practice for states to ensure that they remain under their control and ownership. In negotiating these contracts, prospective licensees should appreciate that licensors are the real owners of these resources, and that as independent sovereign states, they have bargaining powers.[1] Furthermore, a sovereign state, from a legal standpoint, is stronger than a licensee, which is usually a transnational corporation, a private corporation, incorporated in a foreign jurisdiction.

The gradual transformation of the negotiation process for petroleum and mining contracts, which is noteworthy, may be shown at different periods since 1900:1900–44; 1945–55; 1956–75. In the following section, in justifying the division of these periods, the changing pattern of negotiation techniques has also been discussed.

9.1.1 1900–44

It is immaterial whether this period started earlier or later than 1900, as it represents the pre-United Nations period, when most of the owners of these resources were colonies. During this period oil concessions were granted to major oil companies with effective control by them of the entire range of petroleum activities, during both the exploration and exploitation stages. The owner (the state in the form of a colony) had the effective control over the foreign corporation and could not participate in the management or the corporation and the resources. The owner (the licensor) simply received an

Negotiation of Petroleum Contracts 133

agreed royalty. Furthermore, large areas used to be allocated to licensees by owners of natural resources to foreign corporations for extremely long periods of time (up to 99 years), without much restriction. Of course, in most cases, the status of the owner as a colony, contributed to this state of affairs. The question of their exerting any bargaining power did not arise. Award of such long-term favourable licences allowed foreign corporations long-term benefits, including an assured income, and even the governing law of the contracts (licences) was the law of the home country of the licensee.

9.1.2   1945-55

This is a crucial period in that with the setting up of the United Nations, the right of self-determination of peoples was affirmed. In other words, the policy of decolonisation of the former colonies was declared to be an avowed policy of the United Nations. This marked the beginning of a new phenomenon, which, over the years, developed various dimensions, reflecting the aspirations of the newly-born states. The right of self-colonisation of the former colonies. Furthermore, the newly-born states considered the Principles and Policies of the United Nations in this respect as contributory to their aspirations.

9.1.3   1956-65

This is the period during which most of the former colonies attained political independence. But political independence without economic emancipation is almost meaningless. Unsurprisingly, the newly-born states wanted a reaffirmation of their ownership in and the right of control over their national resources. This was the origin of the taking of foreign assets, including the oil companies engaged in exploitation activities in the former colonies. But, unpalatable as it may sound, this phenomenon was inevitable. Of course, no sensible international lawyer should support the taking of foreign assets; simply the inevitability of it is to be recognised. However, the developing countries did not wish to depart from the customary rule of international law whereby the duty of payment of compensation is sacrosanct. This was reaffirmed by the UN General Assembly Resolution entitled Permanent Sovereignty over Natural Resources, 1962.

Paragraph 8 of the Resolution also provides that:

> Foreign investment agreements freely entered into by, or between sovereign States shall be observed in good faith; States and international organisations

shall strictly and conscientiously respect the sovereignty of peoples and nations over their natural wealth and resources in accordance with the Charter and the principles set forth in the present resolution.[2]

This provision identified the need for foreign investment agreements to be freely entered into, that is, without any coercion or prompting from foreign investors; but such investment agreements must be observed in good faith, that is, the principle of *pacta sunt servanda*, must be respected by the contracting parties. Furthermore, the sovereignty of peoples and nations over their natural wealth and resources must be respected. Strictly speaking, this provision, and the Resolution generally, did not suggest anything novel; such principles were already being observed by the developed states in relation to the foreign investment agreements they entered into with foreign corporations. The Resolution simply affirmed it so that foreign investors did not disregard the right of peoples and nations over their natural resources. This Resolution has been accepted by both developed and developing states; indeed, in dealing with cases of taking of foreign assets by host countries, tribunals have relied upon this Resolution too, where foreign assets were taken by states in the national interest.[3] Paragraph 4 of the Resolution provides, inter alia, that:

> Nationalisation, expropriation or requisitioning shall be based on grounds or reasons of public utility, security or the national interest which are recognised as overriding purely individual or private interests, both domestic and foreign. In such cases the owner shall be paid appropriate compensation, in accordance with the rules in force in the State taking such measures in the exercise of its sovereignty and in accordance with international law.

In the arbitration between *Texaco and the Libyan Arab Republic*, Libya invoked the provisions of article 2(c) of the Charter of Economic Rights and Duties of States, 19741 in its attempt to avoid payment of any compensation, but rejecting the Libyan argument, the Arbitrator emphasised that:

> Resolution 1803 (XVII) of 14 December 1962 was passed by the General Assembly by 87 votes to 2, with 12 abstentions. It is particularly important to note that the majority voted for the text, including many States of the Third World, but also several Western developed countries with market economies, including the most important one, the United States. The principles stated in this Resolution were therefore assented to by a great many States representing not only all geographical areas but also all economic systems.[4]

Negotiation of Petroleum Contracts 135

The Arbitrator maintained that provisions of article 2(c) of the Charter of Economic Rights and Duties of States, 1974 were nonrepresentative of the intention of the international community, and pointed out that:

> The conditions under which Resolution 3281 (XXIX), proclaiming the Charter of Economic Rights and Duties of States, was adopted also show unambiguously that there was no general consensus of the States with respect to the most important provisions and in particular those concerning nationalisation. Having been the subject of U.N. General Assembly Resolution 3281 (XXIX) of 1974 matter of a roll-call vote, the Charter was adopted by 118 votes to 6, with 10 abstentions. The analysis of votes on specific sections of the Charter is most significant in so far as the present case is concerned. From this point of view, paragraph 2(c) of Article 2 of the Charter, which limits consideration of the characteristics of compensation to the State and does not refer to international law, was voted by 104 to 16 with 6 abstentions, all of the industrialised countries with market economies having abstained or having voted against it.[5]

The validity of the taking of foreign assets in the national interest and the obligation to pay compensation under customary international law were reaffirmed. Of course, the thorny questions remain who determines 'national interest' and what is 'national interest'. But these cannot be answered by any legal rationale. One must rely upon the validity of the decision of the host state on these issues.[6]

This was also the period during which two identifiable developments took place: (a) the rise of state contracts; and (b) the recognition of economic human rights. In fact, the consequence of the second development became particularly evident during the next decade, i.e., 1966–75. This was the decade when negotiators were required to change their perceptions of ownership and control over the natural resources belonging to foreign states.

9.1.4   1966–75

With the advent of the oil crisis, which was occasioned by multifarious causes, political, economic etc., the aspiration of developing countries for a new international economic order became even more manifest during this period. It is worth pointing out that during the period 1969–74, 16 resolutions, whether relating to financial transactions, monetary issues, economic human rights or private foreign investments, were adopted by the United Nations.[7] But, perhaps the most important ones in the context of this discussion were the Declaration on the Establishment of a New International Economic Order, 1974[8] and the

Programme of Action on the Establishment of a New International Economic Order, 1974. Although many of these resolutions have not been fully adopted by the international community, their influence on the minds of a large number of states may not be disregarded. Developing countries made their aspirations as to economic self-sufficiency with control over private foreign investors. Indeed, this was what negotiators of private foreign investment contracts were required to bear in mind. These resolutions also deliver clearly the message that the developing countries are conscious of the fact that whereas they own vast amounts of natural resources, they also require the assistance of private foreign investors for their exploration and exploitation, but always with their participation. Negotiation of private foreign investment agreements, particularly in the natural resources sectors, is primarily concerned with identifying the bases for mutual cooperation and mutual benefit for both parties, the foreign investor and the host country.

This period consolidated the new pattern of negotiating techniques applicable to agreements relating to the exploration and exploitation of natural resources. Most of the developing countries have now adopted investment legislation and sectorised economies, establishing the 'closed' and 'open' sectors. Many changes to the old-fashioned contractual terms have taken place, such as curtailment of the period of licence (currently licences are granted for a period between eight and 25 years); participation in management and control; restrictive exploitation policy; awareness as to the protection of the environment etc.

The incidence of the taking of private foreign assets in the developing world diminished as from 1980.[9] In fact, in many countries, the privatisation process has already commenced.[10] Negotiators will profit more by accepting the new and inevitable changes that have occurred in the developing world, rather than proceeding with any preconceived idea and undue apprehension of risks. The reality of risks in private foreign investments has already been discussed in chapter 3 of this work.

9.2 The Principal Features of State Contracts

Before discussing the technique of negotiating petroleum contracts, it would be appropriate to identify some of the principal features of state contracts, which a negotiator may find useful. A state contract is a contract to which one party is a government, and the other a private foreign entity, usually, a transnational corporation. It has already been explained in the previous section that during the immediate post-independence period, the governments of the newly independent states found it necessary to regain ownership in their natural resources.

Consequently, it became obvious that to any contract relating to the exploration and exploitation of natural resources, governments would be parties. The participation of a government or a government-sponsored entity as a contracting party, in effect, imports certain special features in such contracts. First, the objective of a state contract is different from that of a traditional commercial contract; the former has, as its objective, welfare of the state, the latter, profit-making; second, the contracting parties are unequal in status – one (the government or the government-sponsored entity) is stronger than the other (the private entity); whereas the government entity can legislate and make the foreign investor subject to it, the private foreign entity cannot do so; third, whereas the state party owes a responsibility towards its nationals for achieving economic development, the private foreign entity primarily performs its contractual obligations in consideration of a monetary profit; fourth, a state contract entails a combination of public law and private law.

But, how to classify a state contract? State contracts are primarily economic development agreements; they are neither treaties, nor are they purely commercial contracts *stricto sensu*. They are a hybrid between a treaty and a traditional commercial contract. They may be described as contracts *sui generis* (a class by themselves).[11] These special features of state contracts should be borne in mind in negotiating petroleum contracts particularly with developing countries.

It would be appropriate to summarise some of the important issues which negotiators are usually required to deal with in negotiating a petroleum exploration and exploitation contract ownership and equity participation; duration of contracts; royalties and other payments; relinquishment; pricing; taxation; training and employment of nationals; transfer of technology; marketing; refining activity; and financing.

These issues are very much related to the phenomenon of awareness of developing countries of ownership and control over their natural resources. A negotiator is required to appreciate this phenomenon and proceed with negotiation accordingly.

It is to be emphasised however in this connection that at present the differences in basic contractual terms between an exploration and exploitation agreement concluded between two rich countries and that between a rich and a poor country are minimal.

9.3 Principal Contractual Terms in a Petroleum Agreement

9.3.1 Ownership and Equity Participation

The ownership issue basically takes three forms: (i) ownership in the form of joint ventures between the foreign company and the state oil company (a common practice in the Middle East and the UK); (ii) ownership vested in the state and production-sharing contracts are concluded; and (iii) mixed or quasi-arrangement, whereby ownership is vested in the state, but in the agreement between the state oil company and the foreign company, 51 per cent equity participation of the latter is retained. The system of wide participating rights for state oil corporations is also prevalent in the developed world.

Ownership automatically allows the state oil corporation to retain control over its natural resources, and business affairs; furthermore, participation of the state oil corporation in the control and management is thus facilitated. Equity participation during the initial stage of the contract is not usually possible for most of the developing countries, but by contractual arrangement their participation in equity is secured over a period of time. It is not difficult to appreciate why ownership combined with equity participation is so important for retaining control over one's own natural resources. In most countries, legislation at present provides for such a mechanism for retaining control over their natural resources.[12]

9.3.2 Duration of Contracts

Since 1956, in particular, a remarkable change of pattern in respect of duration of contracts has taken place; the reason for this change has already been explained in the first part of this chapter. Duration is much shorter than it used to be prior to 1945. Durations for exploration and exploitation are different: whereas the primary exploration period can vary between three and eight years, with a provision for a short extension, a period between 15 and 25 years is normally allowed for exploitation. A short extension (5–6 years) may be allowed to exploitation. It is however possible for parties to negotiate a period for exploration (e.g. in Nigeria), but in most cases clear-cut policies indicating permissible periods for exploration and exploitation of petroleum have been developed. Foreign negotiators should therefore familiarise themselves with the policy of the host country prior to their embarking upon any negotiation.

9.3.3 Royalties and Other Payments

Royalty is a payment on production. It has a long history: in the early days owners of petroleum gave away all powers of control and management of these resources against royalty. Royalty is independent of the net profits. It is generally calculated on posted price, or a reference price based on a weighted average of export prices of crude oil. It can be substituted for oil too. The rule of royalty, in current practice, varies between 10 and 20 per cent. It may also be fixed in relation to production of oil (e.g. in Norway). In addition to royalty, provision for cash bonuses is often made in contracts. In certain countries, cash bonuses are compulsory. Such bonuses are usually paid at signature and at various levels of production. Negotiators should ascertain the level of such bonuses beforehand.

The rate of rentals, another form of payment, is usually low. In addition to an annual rental, an agreed charge per square kilometre is made. The time of payment of rentals may vary from country to country. In this connection, it would be appropriate to define briefly the various financial terms that are used in relation to petroleum contracts. *Cash bonus*, usually cash, a one-time payment, royalty and tax. These are calculated either on the basis of realised price or on posted price. Payment of royalty to an owner of oil does not exempt the concessionaire or licensee from paying statutory income tax to the state revenue authorities. *Realised price* represents the actual price at which a transaction takes place with a third party (price of a barrel of oil). *Surface rent* is payable annually, and is assessed in relation to the area of the concession. It is deducted from royalty as soon as commercial exploitation begins.

9.3.4 Relinquishment

Phasal relinquishment of obligations during the exploration period is a common phenomenon in respect of petroleum agreements. Usually 50 per cent of the original area at the end of the primary term of four to six years is relinquished. This pattern is progressively followed. In certain countries the first stage of relinquishment can be greater than 50 per cent.

9.3.5 Pricing

Pricing and royalty are interconnected issues. Crude oil prices are usually based on actual sales price realised or posted price (set by the host country) which is higher than the actual sales price realised. The price of crude oil is often set at an approximate weighted average of international crude oil prices. Reference price is an important issue in pricing of oil. Reference prices represent the prices set by producing countries by reference to an average of crude oil export prices.

Of course, it is possible for national oil companies to establish their own pricing system, but no price should be significantly different from the average crude oil export prices. Countries belonging to intergovernmental bodies, such as the Organisation for Petroleum Exporting Countries (OPEC), may be required to adopt the prices fixed by such organisations.

9.3.6 Taxation

Many countries operate a special tax called tax on petroleum-based income or some other designated tax. As tax affects incomes, negotiators should ascertain the tax implications of the incomes of the foreign investor before embarking upon actual negotiation. Attention should also be paid to excess profits as a deduction item against the taxable income.

9.3.7 Training and Employment of Nationals

Provisions for training may be left to the discretion of the state oil company (by means of a contract) or they may be clearly stipulated in the contract. Training programmes are often incorporated in a separate agreement. They may also be organised jointly by the foreign investor and the host party. It has become common practice to stipulate that the foreign company must accord preference to eligible local employees in the company.

Whereas certain countries require that a stipulated percentage of profits be allocated to research and training programmes, others provide for spending a stipulated amount on scholarships and educational institutions, which will cater for the required training of chosen personnel. Negotiators should know the legislative and other provisions before embarking upon negotiation of this term.

9.3.8 Transfer of Technology

Various issues regarding transfer of technology have been discussed in a separate chapter in this work. In the petroleum sector, owners, as a matter of practice, seek technology from foreign firms, and transnational corporations possess considerable expertise in relation to transfer of technology.

A transfer of technology contract and the training programme contract are often required to be considered together.

9.3.9 Marketing

Two types of practice have become evident in this regard. In certain countries the state authorities engage foreign companies (that have already been employed for exploitation of oil) to do marketing for oil, whereas in other countries, such as the UK, marketing of oil may be undertaken by the state authority.

9.3.10 Refining Activity

Setting up refineries entails considerable expenditure. Negotiators should prepare a proper feasibility study before discussing this issue. If the production of oil remains at a low level, it may not be profitable for either party (government or the foreign company) to be engaged in this venture. On the other hand, Indonesian petroleum legislation provides that a designated percentage of the foreign oil company's entitlement is to be refined in Indonesia, and that the oil company should construct refineries if none exists. If the host country's consumption and export levels of refined oil are high, it may be worthwhile becoming engaged in such an activity.

9.3.11 Financing

Finance may be made available by various sources: international agencies, such as the International Bank for Reconstruction and Development, or the International Finance Corporation, or an intergovernmental agency, namely the Organisation of Arab Petroleum Exporting Countries or by syndicates. Governments often provide finance for exploitation of oil to secure supplies of crude oil. The construction of the Trans-Andean Pipeline in Peru was financed by Japan in return for a stipulated quantity of oil to Japan for a designated period of time. Negotiators should be familiar with the technique of obtaining finance from these institutions. Usually, it is for the host country to seek finance from all probable sources.

9.4 Some General Comments on International Petroleum Contracts

It may generally be maintained that except for the United States and a small number of other countries, in which private ownership in mineral rights prevails, the majority of states in the world, in practice, maintain a public ownership policy of mineral rights. As explained earlier, the doctrine of state sovereignty over natural resources contributes to this practice.

Indeed, in most of the countries, national oil companies have been set up and the oil regime is governed by the state as the owner. National oil companies are not only the policy-making institutions, but are also the regulatory bodies for petroleum operations. The rules laid down by them serve, in the main, the following purposes:

(i) to control and supervise exploration and exploitation of oil, including production programmes;
(ii) to maximise oil revenue for the state;
(iii) to ensure implementation of prudent exploitation practice, including protection of the environment;
(iv) to ensure that sufficient production is available for domestic consumption;
(v) to choose appropriate operators;
(vi) to ensure that the operator uses the agreed national materials and services; and
(vii) to ensure that incomes from the petroleum sector contribute to the economic development process in the country.

In the developed oil-producing countries, the national oil companies acquire technical expertise, and when such companies form joint ventures with other foreign companies (e.g. joint ventures for the exploitation of North Sea Oil), the national oil companies usually take the supervisory role (with at least 51 per cent participation) and participate in the board's management. They also, in conjunction with the foreign company, increase their downstream involvement and overseas investment. In the case of developing oil-producing countries, the national oil companies, which are usually unable to take a large share in equity participation, gradually increase their participation in order to acquire effective control over the industry. The foreign company however remains responsible for technical and advisory services. It also remains responsible for marketing activities. In other words, the concept of joint venture in this area, is different between developed and developing oil producing countries. In certain of the Middle Eastern countries, ownership is total for the national oil companies, whereas in certain other countries, in Africa, for example, production-sharing (with a high percentage on the side of the state) has become evident. In Peru, the national oil company retains the option to buy, at a negotiated price, part of the interest held by the contractor. Indonesia also favours production-sharing contracts.

It is interesting to note that most of the developing oil-producing countries trade in crude oil, which rich countries require. Joint ventures between national oil companies in the developing oil producing countries and foreign companies as operators and contractors, such as Petrobras in Brazil, increase expertise in both exploration and exploitation activities.

As the setting up of refineries entails considerable costs, many of the developing oil producing countries cannot afford such costs, and even if they can, it is not certain whether such investments will prove to be sufficiently profitable. Nevertheless, attempts at setting up small refineries were made by Chad and Sudan during the 1970s. The Chad programme, before being finalised, encountered a number of obstacles, namely, financial, market-related, price-related etc.; however, it was finally set up with the help of the World Bank. It is to be emphasised that very well-thought out feasibility studies are required prior to implementing such capital-intensive programmes. Most of the developing oil-producing countries are not however in a position now to set up oil refineries, in consequence of which foreign oil companies will mostly be engaged in providing technical, advisory and marketing services, in addition to exploration and exploitation work.

On the basis of state practice in this area, it is possible to draw certain conclusions, which negotiators may find useful.

(a) State participation, at least to the extent of 50–51 per cent, is common. Depending upon the governing legislation, the extent of participation may be higher.
(b) state participation on the boards of management with equal representation by both parties is common.
(c) An extension of the exploration period from four to six years is normally at the discretion of the national oil company. In the absence of a commercial discovery, the exploration agreement must come to an end.
(d) Relinquishment to the extent of a minimum of 25 per cent of the original area at the end of each two years of the contract is common practice, although provisions for accelerated or larger relinquishments are made.
(e) All exploration costs are to be borne by the foreign oil company; the national oil company may pay for its share of the development costs on

commercial discovery or arrange financing by the oil company, with interest thereon, or from outside sources.

(f) In respect of production-sharing contracts, exploration and exploitation costs are usually met by the contractor, and recovered out of production.

(g) Increase of royalty payments is gradual (perhaps, where possible, the maximum should be fixed at the point of negotiation). Of course, in the AMINOIL case, the Government of Kuwait demanded higher royalty in a progressive manner in conformity with the general trend as developed by various Agreements, such as the Tehran Agreement or the Geneva Agreements.

(h) Provision for higher profits in consequence of higher prices and the tax-related issues.

(i) Provision for bonus payments upon commercial discovery and higher production levels.

(j) Provision for supply to the domestic market.

(k) Service contracts, whereby foreign oil companies receive a fee for their services and gain access to assured supplies of oil at market prices, are more prevalent than any other types of contract.

(l) Production-sharing has its advantages in that it is a flexible system in which the national oil company can earn an increased revenue from rising prices, and the contractor may be assured of a fair rate of return.

(m) A concession system also admits of flexibility but it contains fixed terms of reference, especially where it is legislated; the legislative provisions should be carefully studied. (The concession system adopted by Norway, which is different from that adopted prior to the 1950s or 1960s seems to be popular).

(n) It is possible to combine the concession system and the production-sharing system.

9.5 Conclusions

Since the 1970s, the contract-practice in the petroleum sectors has become consolidated, in consequence of which the ownership issue and the authority to control and participate in the management have not given rise to any serious problems. It is believed that a mutual understanding of the owner's aspirations and the aims of the foreign company is essential, and that negotiators should not proceed with any preconceived ideas in negotiating petroleum contracts on behalf of contractors and operators.

Notes

1. Oil in certain limited number of countries belongs to the public sector.
2. U.N. General Assembly Resolution 1803 (XVII).
3. See for example, the arbitrations between *Texaco and the Libyan Arab Republic* (1979) 53 *International Law Reports* 389; *The Government of the State of Kuwait and the American Independent Oil Company* 21 *International Legal Materials* (1982) 976; and *AGIP and The Popular Republic of the Congo (ICSD Arbitration)* 21 *International Legal Materials* (1982) 726.
4. 53 *International Law Reports* (1979) op. cit., at 487.
5. Ibid., at 489.
6. This issue has been discussed in chapter 3 of this work.
7. United Nations General Assembly Resolution A'Res. 3201 (5–VI) of 1 May 1974.
8. Ibid.
9. This issue has been discussed in detail in chapter 3 of this work.
10. For example, India and Zambia.
11. Vedross described them as 'quasi-international agreements'; see further A. Vedross, 'Quasi-international Agreements and International Economic Transactions', 18 *Year Book of World Affairs* (1964) 230–47.
12. See also the UN Code of Conduct on Transnational Corporations, 1992, which is, in effect a resolution of the UN General Assembly. However, this Code of Conduct, and its previous version (1984), which was in draft form, seem to have influenced the drafting of investment legislation in many countries.

10 The Role of the Lawyer in Negotiating International Commercial Contracts: Some Comments

10.1 Introduction

All successful negotiations should end in concluding contracts. Although legal assistance is certainly necessary for the drafting of contracts, it should be pointed out that the hard commercial negotiations should be allowed to be done by the non-lawyer members of a team. The lawyer's function is to study the terms the other members of the team would like to include and clarify the legal implications of those terms and conditions to the parties. Of course, each party will have a lawyer on its team and the final drafting of the contract becomes the joint work of the lawyers. In the case of institutional contracting, such as the loan agreements to which the International Bank for Reconstruction and Development is a party, or where standard forms developed by various institutions are followed, such as FIDIC, the work of the lawyers becomes minimal.

Depending upon the nature of the contract, a lawyer is required to prepare his/her documents, for example, in the case of a project financing or construction contract, a lawyer must understand the stages and complexities involved in the contractual arrangements and prepare documents accordingly. In general, however, a lawyer must enquire into certain basic issues in drafting any international commercial contract.

(a) The status of the contracting parties – whether government or government-sponsored bodies, and whether the individual signing the contract has the legal capacity and authority to do so. This issue is particularly important when a constituent state as a unit of the federal authority signs a contract. The federal authority's approval is usually required for the contract to be enforceable.

(b) In the case of a government party, the political status of the government (whether it is a recognised or unrecognised government), its political, economic and financial record.

(c) The question of the stability of the government, and if the government changes whether devolution of obligation on the successor government may be possible.

(d) The nature of foreign exchange regulations in the host country, and in what way(s) these regulations may affect the contract, with precautionary measures to be taken accordingly.

(e) The general business environment and the relevant legislation, namely, company law, tax law, commercial law generally, labour law etc.

(f) In the case of an investment contract, the investment legislation and the past record of treatment of foreign investors.

(g) In the case of export sales, the import prohibitory regulations, and the regulations that may prevent the buyer from remitting funds abroad or issuing import licences.

(h) The issue of 'waiver' of sovereign immunity when a contracting party is a government department or a government-sponsored body.

(i) Warranties as to the true disclosure of information by the parties.

(j) Product liability issues, where relevant.

(k) Intellectual property related issues, where relevant.

(l) Certificate(s) of quality of product or goods, where relevant.

(m) Principal-agency relationship, the issues of assignment, novation etc., where relevant.

(n) Whether the contract which is being concluded will be regarded as a valid and enforceable contract in the jurisdictions of both parties.

(o) The issue of cession, annexation of territories. This issue is important in the case of mining and manufacturing products.

(p) Security arrangements in the case of loan agreements.

The list of what a lawyer should take into consideration in drafting contracts cannot be exhausted. Depending upon the nature of the subject matter of the contract, a lawyer is required to consider the legal issues and take precautionary measures against risks on behalf of his/her claim.

10.2 Jurisdictional Issues and Governing Law

Issues relating to jurisdiction and the governing law often create legal problems. Traditionally, almost as a matter of practice, the jurisdiction and the law of the seller, lender, investor, as the case may be, used to be chosen. During the colonial period and until about the mid-1960s, generally, this practice persisted. The notion that the legal systems of the British Commonwealth of Nations were largely influenced by the English common law seems to have contributed to this practice. The same is true of the contracts between France and the Francophone countries.

Since the mid-1960s however, this practice has been questioned by many states. The opposite, that is, to choose the jurisdiction and governing law of the host country, borrower, buyer etc. will not offer an appropriate solution either, as both represent extremities. Choice thus made runs counter to the principle of equality of parties.

Secondly, the principle of the freedom of parties is perhaps theoretical in many respects: parties often do not comprehend the complexity of choosing the jurisdiction and the governing law of their contracts. Therefore, in the final analysis in most cases, it is the lawyer who chooses them on behalf of their clients.

The choice of a national jurisdiction and a national law as the governing law of an international commercial contract has its own problems; their applicability may be questioned by a party. A lawyer may therefore like to consider whether the choice of a neutral jurisdiction and a neutral law, such as the general principles, of law recognised by states may not be more appropriate. Disputes arising under state contracts have been settled by arbitral tribunals by applying general principles of law recognised by states.[1] Of course, where characterisation of contracts becomes important, such as letters of credit contracts, it is recognised that the place of negotiation of the credit/payment gives the jurisdiction and the governing law. In the case of syndicated loan agreements, the current practice is to choose the jurisdiction and the governing law of the country in which the loan has been arranged, which is in most cases, English law (London being the Eurodollar centre) or the law of New York, as many such agreements are concluded in New York.

Reference of a dispute to a third country amounts to delocalising the contract. Delocalisation is the first stage to neutralising a contract, and perhaps advantage should be taken of it by applying a neutral law such as the general principles of law recognised by states, which are identifiable, and which also contains principles of procedure, to ensure that the dispute has been settled

The Role of the Lawyer in Negotiating International Commercial Contracts 149

by a totally neutral mechanism. Thus the enforceability of the awards may also be secured.

10.3 Conclusions

The choice of law issue is a particularly difficult issue. The purpose is not to criticise the traditional practice developed in determining the jurisdiction and the governing law of a transnational commercial contract, but to point out the controversy that has become manifest over recent years. Article 42 of the Convention on the Settlement of Investment Disputes between States and Nationals of Other States, 1965, which is enforced for settling investment disputes between a state and a transnational corporation, provides for rules of international law and the general principles of law recognised by statutes, in addition to other choices too. It is an area of law which should receive the urgent attention of practising lawyers.

Note

1 See, for example, *B.P. Exploration Co. (Libya) Ltd. v. Government of the Libyan Arab Republic* (1979) 53 *International Law Reports* 297; and *Texaco Overseas Petroleum Co. and California Asiatic Oil Co. v. The Government of the Libyan Arab Republic*, ibid., at 389; see also R.Y. Jennings, 'State Contracts in International Law', *British Yearbook of International Law* (1961) 156, and McNair (Lord) 'The General Principles of Law Recognised by Civilised Nations', *British Yearbook of International Law* (1957), 1.

Bibliography

Acams, J. (ed.), *Schmitthoff's Export Trade: The Law And Practice Of International Trade*, London, Stevens & Sons (1990).

Arora, A., 'The Legal Position Of Bonds And Performance Bonds', *Lloyd's Maritime and Commercial Law Quarterly* (1981).

Brierly, J., *Law Of Nations*, Oxford, Clarendon Press, 6th edn.

Chatterjee, C., *Legal Aspects Of Transnational Marketing and Sales*, London, Cavendish (1996).

Chatterjee, S.K., 'The Convention Establishing The Multilateral Investment Guarantee Agency', 36 *International and Comparative Law Quarterly* (1987), 76–91.

Chatterjee, S.K., 'The Charter Of Economic Rights And Duties Of States: An Evaluation After 15 Years', 40 *International and Comparative Law Quarterly* (1991), 669–84.

Chatterjee, S.K., 'The World Bank' in *International Economic Law and Developing States*, Vol. II, London, The British Institute Of International And Comparative Law (1992).

Chatterjee, S.K., 'Procedural Aspects Of Project Finance', 10 *Journal of International Banking Law* (1993), 421–5.

Cohen, H., 'The Responsibility Of The Successor State For War Debts', 44 *American Journal of International Law* (1950), 477.

Condoy-Sekes, R., *Techniques Of Privatisation Of State-Owned Enterprises: Inventory Of Country Experience*, Vol. II, Washington, DC, World Bank (1988).

Fitzmaurice, G., 'State Immunity From Proceedings In Foreign Courts,' 14 *British Year Book of International Law*, 101–24.

Glade, W., *Privatisation Of Public Enterprises In America*, San Francisco, International Center For Economic Growth (1991).

Hawkins, R.G. and Provissiero, N., 'Government Takeovers Of U.S. Foreign Affiliates', 7 *Journal of International Business Studies* (1976), 3–16.

Holman, R., 'Zambia's Privatisation Program,' *Wall Street Journal*, March (1993).

Jennings, R.Y., 'State Contracts In International Law,' *British Year Book of International Law* (1961), 156.

Jodice, D., 'Sources Of Change In Third World Regimes For Foreign Direct Investment 1968–76', 34 *International Organization* (1980), 177–206.

Kamn, T., 'Argentina Offers YPF SA to Local Foreign Investors', *Wall Street Journal*, June (1993).

Kikeri, S., Nellis, J. and Shirley, M., *Privatisation: The Lessons of Experience*, Washington, DC, The World Bank (1992).

Korbin, S.J., 'Foreign Enterprises and Forced Divestment in the LDCs', 34 *International Organization* (1980), 65–88.
Kramer, L., *Focus on European Environmental Law*, London, Sweet & Maxwell (1992).
Lalive, P., 'Swiss Law and Practice in Relation to Measures of Execution against the Property of a Foreign State', 10 *Netherlands Year Book of International Law* (1979), 153.
Lang, W., Neuhold, H. and Zemanek, K., *Environmental Protection and International Law*, London, Graham & Trotman (1991).
Lauterpacht, H., 'The Problem of Jurisdictional Immunities of Foreign States', 28 *British Year Book of International Law* (1951), 225.
McNair, Lord, 'The General Principles of Law Recognised by Civilised Nations', 34 *British Year Book of International Law* (1957), 1.
Minor, M., *Privatisation: a Worldwide Summary*, Report prepared for the Transnational Corporations and Management Division of the United Nations, New York, UN (1993).
Minor, M., 'The Demise of Expropriation as an Instrument of LDC Policy, 1980–1992', 25 *Journal of International Business Studies* (1994), 177.
Penn, G., Shea, A.M. and Arora, A., *The Law and Practice of International Banking*, Vol. 2, London, Sweet & Maxwell (1987).
Ramamurti, R., 'Why are Developing Countries Privatising?', 23 *Journal of International Business Studies* (1992), 225.
Ramamurti, R. and Vernor, R. (eds), *Privatisation and Control of State-owned Enterprises*, Washington, DC, The World Bank (1991).
Shelton, D., *International Environmental Law*, London, Transnational Publishers Inc. (1991).
Solis, D., 'As Mexico's Pemex nears Privatisation, Foreign Energy Firms Gear up to Drill', *Wall Street Journal*, August (1992).
Tanner, J., 'Venezuela Starts to bring back Foreign Oil Firms', *Wall Street Journal*, March (1993).
UN Centre on Transnational Corporations, *Trends in Forced Divestment of Foreign Affiliates, 1960–1979*, Report of the UNCTC (1982), 13.
Vedross, A., 'Quasi-international Agreements and International Economic Transactions', 18 *Year Book of International Affairs* (1964), 230.
Vuylsteke, C., *Techniques of Privatisation of State-owned Enterprises, Vol.1: Methods and Implementation*, Washington, DC, The World Bank (1988).
Wallace, L., 'MIGA: Up and Running', *Finance and Development* (1992), 48.

Index

abandonment 19, 20
absolute immunity 87-8
advance warning system 93
African Development Bank 39
aggressiveness 3, 4
Alcom case 91
Aminoil case 41, 144
ancillary questions 10
annexation of territories 147
assignment 67, 76, 101, 147
assignment of proceeds 75, 77-81
availability date 108

'balloon' payments 93, 105
bargaining power 1, 12, 125, 132-3
blueprint of a project 15, 111
British Commonwealth of Nations 148
'bullet' payments 93, 105
buyback 53, 54

capital goods 59
capital-intensive programme 143
certificate of quality 120
Charter of Economic Rights and Duties of States 134-5
civil wars 38, 128
combat action 38
COMECON countries 52
commencement date 114-15
commercial exploitation 139
Conditions of Contract (International) for Works of Civil Engineering Cons-truction 113
consignee code 63
continuing risks 23
contract factory 61, 63, 66

Convention on the Settlement of Investment Disputes 34, 149
credit rating 17
cultural differences 5, 21
customary international law 17, 33, 41, 135

debentures 100
debt-equity ratios 77
decolonisation 17, 40, 87, 132-3
design 61, 65, 109, 111, 116-17, 129
developing countries 23, 40, 42-3, 52, 71, 96, 133, 135-8
documentary bonds 127
documentary credit mechanism 48
dossier 97, 100
due care and skill 102-3
due diligence 20, 33, 36, 38-9

Eastern Bloc countries 75
enforceable contract 147
environmental education 24
environmental pollution 22, 26, 33-4
equality of parties 148
Euro-currency loans 106
Eurobond market 92, 103
Eurodollar 148
European Convention on State Immunity 90
European Union 17, 29, 30, 32, 49
expert certificate 49, 50
Export Credit Guarantee Department 16
expropriation of assets 16, 40-41, 134

federal authority 90, 146-7
FIDIC 113, 128, 130, 146

financial records 102
fixed costs 62, 104, 117–18, 120
fixed damages 122
foreign exchange regulations 50–51, 73, 78–80, 82, 147
foreseeable risks 37, 42–3
Francophone countries 148
frustration of contracts 128

governing law 49, 68, 83, 107, 128, 130, 133, 148–9
government-backed projects 70, 79, 100, 123, 146–7
government-sponsored entity 99, 104, 129, 137

impossibility of performance 43, 66, 126
incidence of risks 15, 42, 43
incorporated technology 59
indemnity 122
informality 5
International Chamber of Commerce 44, 49, 51, 57, 130
International Development Agency 39
International Finance Corporation 39, 42, 70, 84, 92, 141
International Monetary Fund 15
invitation to tender 112
irrevocable credit 51

jure gestionis 87–9
jure impeii 87–9

lead bank 96–7, 99, 102–3
LIBOR 103–4, 106
licensed product 61, 64–5
licensed sales territory 61
liquidated damages 122
lock-outs 18, 20, 128
London Court of International Arbitration 130
long-term purchasers 79

mandate 5, 10–11, 99
misrepresentation 57, 112
mortgages 76–7, 81, 106
Multilateral Investment Guarantee Agency 16, 42

national debt 79–80, 85–6, 97
national emergency 79
national interest 16–17, 40–41, 79, 134–5
nationalisation 16, 41–2, 134–5
negative attitude 3, 5, 6, 11
negative pledge 77, 81, 83
negligent use of technology 22
new international economic order 135–6
newly-born states 133
novation 101, 147

Organisation for Petroleum Exporting Countries 140
overseas contractor 126
Overseas Private Investment Corporation 16

packaging 47, 63
pacta sunt servanda 40, 86, 134
pari passu 76, 83, 98, 106–7
performance requirements 18, 20
'polluter pays' principle 31, 32
prime rate 104, 106
product liability 47, 121–2, 147
production-sharing contracts 138, 143–4
project cycle 44, 92
promissory note 74
psychological factor 11
punch list 120

registrar of companies 99
renegotiation clause 79
restituto in integrum 41
restrictive covenant 77
restrictive exploitation policy 136
restrictive sovereign immunity 90

revocable credit 51
risk minimisation 72
risky agreement 75

satisfactory quality 57
securities commission 99
self-determination of peoples 133
service contract 144
sponsors 70, 72, 74–5, 78
Sri Lanka 38
state responsibility 23–4, 33, 35
strict liability 33, 35, 39
strikes 18, 20, 128
sub-buyer 51
sub-licensing 65
successor government 78, 85–6, 97–8, 107, 147

team leader 4, 7, 10–13
technical documentation 61–6
technical know-how 61, 64–5
technological self-sufficiency 55
through-put agreements 79
trustee 74, 78–9
turn-key contracts 19, 53–4, 56, 111

United Nations 22, 85, 133, 135

waiver 73, 78, 82, 88–9, 92, 94, 107, 117, 129, 147
warranties 17, 56, 73, 92, 121–2, 128–9, 147
World Bank 16, 92, 99, 143
World Bank Group 54, 70, 84, 92